William T. Bisignani, Ph.D., P.E.

YOUR WORLD, MY WORLD, OUR WORLD

Strategies for Thinking, Planning and Decision Making in a Connected World

ISBN: 1452899509
ISBN-13: 9781452899503

For My Family, My World
With Love Always

ABOUT THE AUTHOR

William T. Bisignani has over 40 years of experience as an information systems management consultant, engineering manager, systems engineer, researcher and university teacher. He has a Ph.D. in Electrical Engineering from Rutgers University and is a licensed professional engineer. He has worked at think tanks, management consulting firms, universities and research laboratories. His specialty areas include information systems, telecommunications, systems thinking and systems engineering, strategic planning, decision theory, visualization, management, and other areas presented in this book. William T. Bisignani has taught over 175 graduate and undergraduate courses at Rutgers University, George Washington University, Florida Gulf Coast University and Edison College. As a Technical Director at the MITRE Corporation and Mitretek Systems, Inc. and as a principal at Booz, Allen and Hamilton, he has interfaced with people at all levels in the business and government communities. His clients included over 40 federal, state and local government organizations where he has applied the concepts in this book in designing and implementing new ways of doing business and solving problems. He has published over 30 management and technical reports in technical journals, and has organized and/chaired over 25 technical conferences. He is a member of the IEEE and AIAA. He can be reached at bisignani@comcast.net.

TABLE OF CONTENTS

PART III – SYSTEMS THINKING AND PROBLEM SOLVING IN MY SYSTEMS WORLD

LIST OF ILLUSTRATIONS

INTRODUCTION

Background

We live in a complex and interconnected world. Every day we interface with *many* people through face-to-face conversations, email, social networks. Every day we try to solve *many* simple and complex problems. Everyday we make *many* decisions. Sometimes we do a good job; more often we could do better. But suppose we have a better understanding of our own individual environment – of our own personal world - and suppose that we have good tools to help us, and suppose that we have step-by-step procedures to follow, and suppose that we have the desire to enrich our lives and the lives of our loved ones, and suppose that we have the strategies to do all these things, then could we do better in the *many* things that we do? Think about it.

I have been using the ideas and techniques presented in this book for many years. These techniques have helped me think strategically, plan my activities and actions, and focus on decisions I am making. Now I look at the world and its everyday challenges differently than I did before and I continue to use these ideas and concepts every day.

This book presents these ideas and concepts to help you, the reader, by providing guidance, strategies and tools to help you plan, make more informed decisions, and identify appropriate actions you could take to get what you want! I introduce you to what I call *Systems Worlds*, to a critical thinking approach called *Systems Thinking*, and to the scientific concepts of systems analysis, systems engineering and decision theory. I meld these disciplines in an easy to understand approach.

You will see that your decisions and actions can affect not only you, but other people - people you love, people you work with, and people that you do not even know. Your actions can affect nature and your environment. Your actions can affect business, even the world economy. Your actions can affect ideas.

Every living organism has its Own Systems World, a world whose elements impact the organism and where the organism impacts its elements. In each organism's world, actions are taken – some conscious, some driven by instinct. For the human organism, these are often complex decisions involving many factors. But we usually make these decisions based on incomplete data or by "gut reaction." There are better ways. I discuss methods to get better results and better control over your own unique environment, which I call *My Systems World*.

After reading this book, I hope that:

- You will look at the world differently.
- You will think differently.
- You will act differently.

It is also important to understand that the ideas and techniques that I present apply equally well to individuals, groups and organizations. These concepts therefore can be used in personal, family, business, government, and educational environments.

Organization of this Book

I have divided the book into three parts.

Part I helps us understand My Systems World. My Systems World helps each of us focus on the parts of our connected world which affect our current and future environments. It helps us understand the consequences of our decisions and actions. My Systems World interacts with many other Systems Worlds, so that the actions we take in My Systems World can affect these other Systems Worlds. The interactions among various Systems Worlds can be minimal or they can be significant.

In Part I, I also describe the concepts of systems and Systems Thinking as a way of thinking about our environment in My Systems World. My approach to systems thinking provides a unique combination of several approaches that have been used in the scientific and educational communities.

Part I leads us to a discussion on making decisions which I explore in more depth in Part II. Essentially everything we do in life involves making decisions. Many decisions appear trivial, but they may have more far reaching effects than we think (e.g., food choices). Some decisions have major impacts both on us and on others. So how can we make better decisions? Part II presents decision making concepts and tools that we can use and helps prioritize tools we should consider for different circumstances.

Part III integrates systems thinking with decision making approaches to help us better function in My Systems World. Part III contains a 5-step approach which we can use to solve many problems that arise in My Systems World. These five key steps are discussed in sufficient detail to permit developing good solutions. These ideas are applied to solving both simple and complex problems in My Systems World.

To make these concepts easier to understand, *Your World, My World, Our World*, makes liberal use of examples, diagrams, and checklists.

I hope you find these ideas interesting and challenging and then apply them in your own Systems World.

PART I
—
SYSTEMS THINKING AND MY SYSTEMS WORLD

CHAPTER 1

IT'S A MAD, MAD, MAD, MAD SYSTEMS WORLD

What's a Person to Think?

Our world is a very complex place. Things are constantly changing. As we think about it, we notice that today's world is different! Different from last year, different from last week, different from yesterday, different from when you began to read this book. It is changing – instant by instant.

The physical planet is changing. Ideas are changing. We are changing. But whenever something changes, it affects many other persons, places, things and ideas. This tells us that many, many things are connected – some by strong connections – some by weak connections.

So how do we react to this changing world – or should we even bother?

It's an overwhelming idea to think that we, as individuals, can affect the whole world by our actions. But we should be able to affect, to some extent, our own local environment. This is what I call *My Systems World*. Extending this idea to groups of people, we can consider any organization as having its own Systems World.

The complexity of a given Systems World will vary significantly from person to person and from organization to organization. Each Systems World also changes over time.

Think about it. Initially when one is born, there is a small group of people and things in the baby's Systems World. Elements in this Systems World include parents, relatives, friends, medical personnel, clothing, crib, and other equipment. As the baby grows, his/her Systems World expands to encompass more and more people, things, places and ideas.

Throughout history, a person's personal Systems World has expanded to include more connections, more things, and more persons. New roads were built. Better transportation capabilities were developed. Better means of communicating were implemented. A person's world was indeed expanded.

In the business world, these improvements permitted expansion of different industries. Fresh produce could be shipped farther. The number of new customers were increased. Many companies grew from local shops to regional companies to global enterprises.

In this book we explore several interrelated concepts: concepts of connectivity, concepts of systems, concepts of decision making, and concepts of problem solving – but throughout them all, concepts of thinking.

Almost everything that we do requires a decision on our part – either consciously or subconsciously. From deciding what to eat for lunch (an action which can have long term consequences) to determining which complex business activities (such as mergers or acquisitions) we need to perform, we need to make decisions. Some are simple "no-brainers". Others require extensive analysis and critical thinking.

This book can train us to think in our complex world – to help us organize our thoughts and make better decisions. It introduces the concept of Systems Thinking as well as a new way of gathering and organizing data that we will need to make these decisions. This approach will lead to the development of our own unique world, our own Systems World. The book combines intuitive methods and methods developed in laboratories and universities and provide new perspectives on how to use these methods. Hence, the information in this book will present us with the ideas and tools that we can use to think clearly and logically and to make good decisions. The approaches presented may at first seem difficult, but after using them, they can become second nature to us.

I Know You and You and You

In 1967 a researcher ran an experiment and formulated the theory called six degrees of separation. Six degrees of separation says that anyone on earth can be connected to any other person on earth through a link of acquaintances with no more than five intermediaries. Although this has not been mathematically proven, it still gives us a feeling that there is some small number of people in a link that can connect two persons. In fact, a TV show entitled "6 Degrees of Martina McBride" was shown where six people from across America are trying to "connect" with country singer Martina McBride. With certain restrictions such as not being able to call her office, attend her concerts, or search for her on the internet, they were to go to someone they knew and ask them to take them to someone that person knew and so on with the goal of getting to someone who knew the singer personally. All six people were successful, some with less than six connections.

Now enter the internet. The internet has connected people from all walks of life and from all parts of the world. It has made it possible to send information almost anywhere in fractions of a second. This internet time, if not reducing the number of intermediaries (which it might do), certainly reduces the time between connecting any two people. So this internet time has changed many things we do and how we do it. Ideas (good and bad) sent over the internet can cause people to quickly change their minds and habits.

Some people try to hasten these connections using internet sites such as My Space, Facebook, LinkedIn or eHarmony which post or make available information submitted by individuals. These social networks further increase connectivity and reduce isolation among individuals.

The internet can be considered a communications system interconnecting all the computers that are attached to it, and by extension, to all the people using these computers. Broadening this concept of a communication system to include other types of systems is the key to developing our knowledge and our decision making skills. Whether we want to or not, we are connected to others through several world-wide systems [for example, transportation systems (includes airplanes and automobiles), telecommunication systems (phone, internet), and ecosystems (water, global weather)]. And although we share some of these world-wide systems, we each have our own unique set of systems in which we interact. As pointed out before, this collection of an individual's systems becomes an integral part of Our Systems World.

So each person has their Own Systems World. I call mine "My Systems World" to distinguish it from everyone else's. Everyone has a "My Systems World." In each person's version of My Systems World there is a collection of systems. But what is a system? To better understand this concept, let's look at a simple definition used for the term system.

A system is a collection of elements (a bunch of things) that work together to achieve some goal.

For example, we each have a human body system. It consists of our respiratory system, our nervous system, our circulatory system, our visual system, our olfactory system, our skeletal system, and so on. For each of us, however, the size and quality of each biological system may vary. Some one may have a visual system with 20/20 vision while someone else may require glasses to correct their vision. Different conditions or diseases may exist in different persons. Hence, each person's human body system in My Systems World will be different than every other person's human body in their Systems World.

Since this concept of a system is so important in understanding My Systems World, I discuss the concept of a system in more detail in

Chapter 2. Also in Chapter 2, I present an example of an individual's Systems World.

Since there are many individual and overlapping systems in each of Our Systems World, we need a way of looking at what we do and why. In Chapters 2 and 3, I introduce the concept of *systems thinking* and suggest that this is the best way to handle the environment in My Systems World.

So, in this book, we look at the world in general and My Systems World in particular using a systems thinking perspective. We develop ways to think about our environment and how various elements in our environment affect our lives. We look at how to prepare ourselves and organize ourselves to function more effectively and efficiently. We look at how to make good decisions, and to solve problems. To help us in performing these activities, I introduce ideas and tools that we can use.

Interconnectivity and Systems go Together As Milk and Honey

One cannot say enough about how each of us is connected to other people and with the environment. Time after time we see that when an action occurs, it can produce changes in actions elsewhere. So these actions are interconnected. Sometimes these actions are important and other times the interaction effects are minor. These interactions occur wherever we are involved - in our business, personal life, finances, education and so on.

Let's go back to a rhyme from centuries ago:

> For want of a nail the shoe was lost
> For want of a shoe the horse was lost
> For want of a horse the rider was lost
> For want of a rider the battle was lost
> For want of a battle the kingdom was lost
> And all for the want of a horseshoe nail.

This is an interesting case of an action producing another action, which produces another action, and so on. We can further say that the horse is a part of a transportation system, the horse and rider are part of a military system, and all the elements in the rhyme are part of a political system. So we see in Figure 1-1 that the transportation system is part of the other two systems (Military System, Political System).

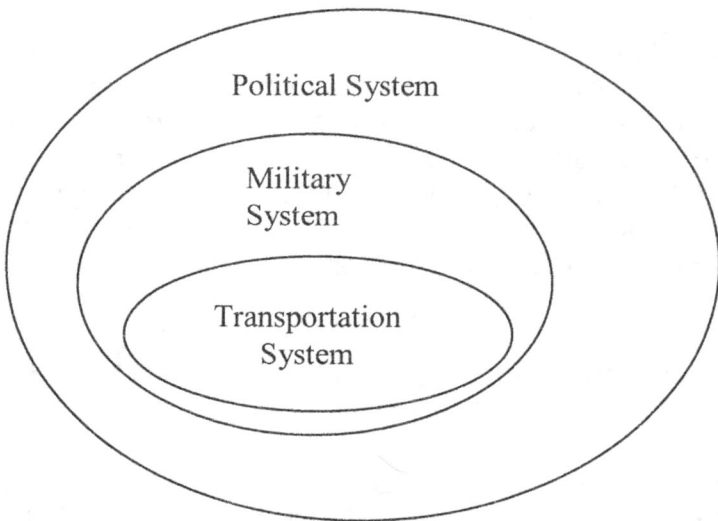

Figure 1-1 - Nesting of Systems

Butterfly Effect - Let's look at another example that appears counterintuitive. You may have heard of the butterfly effect. There was a movie by this name in 2004 with the tag line: Change One Thing, Change Everything. This resulted from research done in the early 1960s by a meteorologist named Edward Lorenz. Lorenz was studying weather prediction methodologies. He found that very small changes in the starting values in the weather models he built resulted in significant changes in the results that occurred later. He equated the small initial changes to the flapping of a butterfly's wings and stated the following:

> The flapping of a single butterfly's wing today produces a tiny change in the state of the atmosphere. Over a period of time, what the atmosphere actually does diverges from what it would have done. So, in a month's time, a tornado that would have devastated the Indonesian coast doesn't happen. Or maybe one that wasn't going to happen, does. (Ian Stewart, Does God Play Dice? The Mathematics of Chaos, pg. 141)

This is an extreme example of interaction, but it illustrates our very important point that many things are linked together – many things that we might not even think about. Something that we do today may have profound effects in the future.

Summary - As we interact with the elements in Our Systems World, we see that there are many ways that we can use these interactions to accomplish incredible things. We might be able to effectively multiply our productivity and knowledge to improve the ways that we live, work, shop and play. We can learn new approaches to decision making and problem solving. We can make more intelligent decisions. Our communications with others can improve. We can collaborate over great distances and, if we act intelligently, can enhance our capabilities in Our Systems World. We can evaluate more clearly the effects we have in preserving our environment and making our great institutions work better. So let's continue to explore these interactions and determine what the concept of systems thinking can do for us and others in Our Systems World.

SYSTEMS, SYSTEMS EVERYWHERE!

A System is a Beautiful Thing

In it basic form, a system is nothing more than several things working together to reach some goal. The things (often called elements or components) as well as the interconnections among them (often called the relationships) are important in determining how the system will react to changes.

The outside or external changes to a system are often called the inputs to the system. The system manipulates the inputs and generates some action (often called an output). This output might also affect the system, in other words, it might feed back some changes to the system. A basic system is shown in the Figure 2-1.

When I talk about My Systems World, I mean knowing that many things in this world are linked or connected in some way, and that we need to take into account these linkages in trying to reach any of our goals. We must be concerned with what we do to the system (what types of inputs we give to the system) and how the system may react to the different inputs.

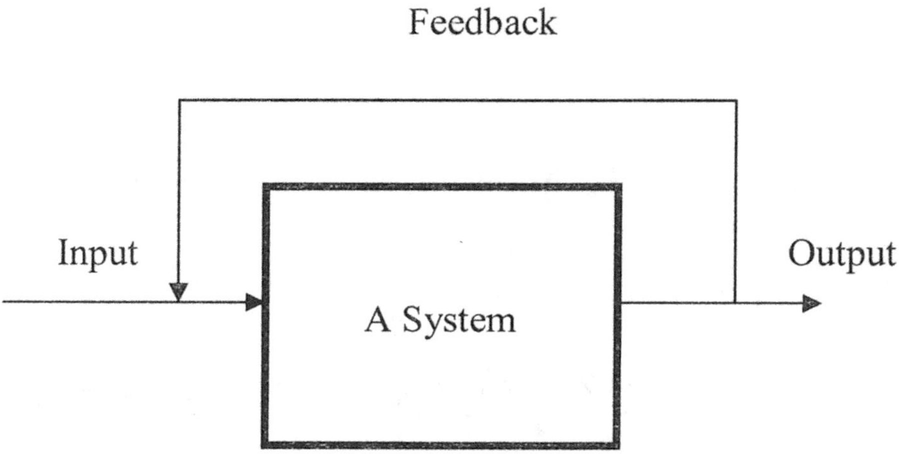

Feedback

Figure 2-1 – A Basic System with input, output and feedback

Let's look at some systems to help us better understand the systems concept.

Honey I Shrank the Air Transportation System

Suppose our goal is to get from New York to San Francisco safely in less than 10 hours. Currently our only viable solution is to use an *Air Transportation System*. Our Air Transportation System consists of at least the following: airplanes, airports, and air traffic control systems. What's interesting about systems is that they are made up of other smaller systems. An airplane is a system. Airplanes themselves have many systems: a navigation system to guide the airplane; a propulsion system to make the airplane go; a control system to control the flight of the airplane; a landing gear system which includes the wheels and tires; a communications system to talk to air traffic controllers and to other airplanes; and so on. All of these systems come together to make up the airplane system whose goal is to carry passengers and cargo safely from one place to another through the air.

Now what kind of inputs can we have to the Air Transportation System? One input is weather. If the weather is bad, this can affect the system. The output of such an input could cause a bumpy ride, or it could cause a late arrival because the plane needed to take an alternate route or perhaps it will require that the flight be cancelled. A cancelled flight might then feedback into the system the inputs requiring that all the passengers be rescheduled on different flights at different times, and so on.

So we have our system being affected by its inputs that may result in different outcomes than our planned goal of arriving in less than 10 hours.

Is BIGGER Better?

We can continue this thinking process for each of the airplane's systems. For example, the propulsion system can be further divided into smaller systems like the engines and its parts such as the rotors, compressors, etc. But what is interesting is that we can also go in the other direction by combining systems to make larger systems. For example, we can include cars and trains and ships to form a General Transportation System. The general transportation system has a goal of moving people and goods from one place to another. Figure 2-2 uses groupings of each of the general transportation systems areas to illustrate this concept. These groupings are called Venn diagrams and we will discuss them in more detail in Chapter 4.

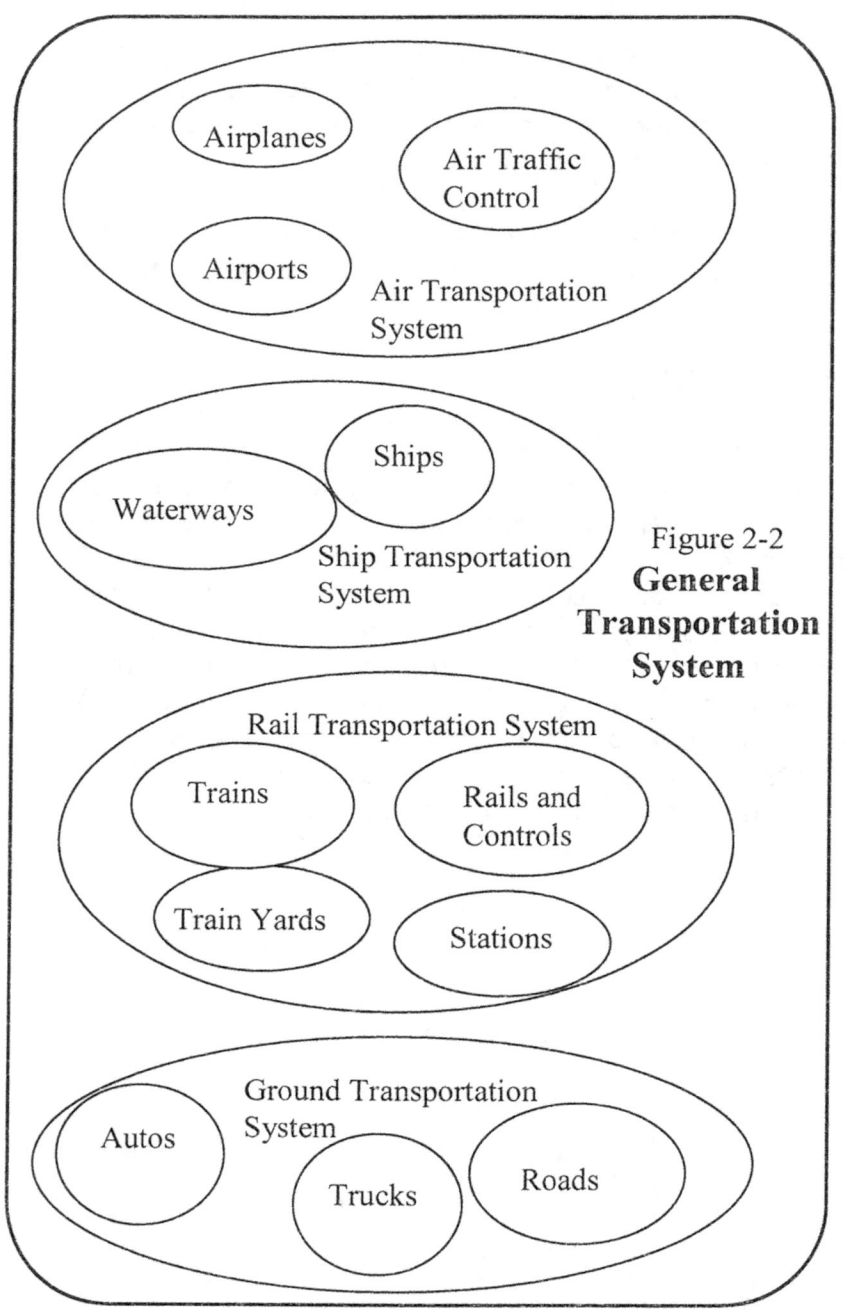

Figure 2-2 – General Transportation System

A System Here, A System There, A System Everywhere

This expansion or contraction of a system is what makes the idea of a system so intriguing. Essentially everything we see when we look around us is both a system by itself as well as a part of a larger system. And each of these systems can be divided into smaller systems. So if we think about it, SYSTEMS ARE EVERYWHERE. Expanding our everyday thinking to view our activities as interacting with systems, then we can start to link our activities and the things around us into more efficient ways to do things. We can link our actions with things (including people) and data and other activities to achieve more and better results in our everyday activities (e.g., at work). In fact, if we think of ourselves and everything we come in contact with as My Systems World, then our decisions and actions can be viewed as affecting My Systems World. Since our actions can affect those around us and if we consider the possible effects from this perspective, we might make different (and hopefully better) decisions and choices.

If you type the word system into any computerized search engine, you will get thousands of hits. A recent search identified many systems that we may interact with on a regular basis. A summary of some of the key responses from the hit list is the following.

- Monetary systems
- Biological systems
- Communications systems
- Information systems
- Business systems
- Mathematical systems
- Systems engineering
- Systems design
- Systems identification
- Solar system
- Interstate highway system
- Columbia Broadcasting System
- Linear systems
- Non-linear systems
- Decimal and metric systems
- U.S. Federal Reserve System

We have a very diverse list to say the least, but it should be clear that there are many types of systems and that we are familiar with many of them. So the concept of developing My Systems World is nothing out of the ordinary – we just have to start to think in the systems world.

Let's discuss a few of these systems in a little more detail. I am just skimming the surface in what I am presenting since each of these systems is composed of many smaller systems.

A Body is a Beautiful (and Complicated) System to Behold

The human body system is an excellent example to illustrate the elements of a system, viz., input, output, feedback and the system itself. We are all familiar with many of the body systems and what they can and cannot do, but let's put some details in the description of the human body system.

The human body is made up of many systems. These include the following:

- Skeletal
- Digestive
- Muscular
- Lymphatic
- Endocrine
- Nervous
- Cardiovascular
- Reproductive
- Urinary

We are familiar with many of the capabilities of each of these systems. Thinking about each of these will start to give us the feeling of the elements of each system.

As an example, let's look at the Digestive System of the human body. Our digestive system by itself is quite complex. The digestive system is mainly made up of the following components (which we can call sub-systems):

- Mouth
- Teeth
- Esophagus
- Stomach
- Liver
- Small Intestine
- Colon
- Gallbladder
- Spleen
- Rectum

Let's look at the digestive system and identify the elements introduced in the definition of a system: input, output, feedback and the system. The input is through the mouth, the output is through the rectum, and feedback occurs through many different mechanisms. For example, we get the feedback identified below when we provide the stated inputs.

- Case 1 - If we eat too much food, our feedback mechanism will tell us that we feel full.
- Case 2 - If we eat spicy foods, we might get indigestion.
- Case 3 - If we eat contaminated foods, we will probably get sick.
- Case 4 - If we drink too many alcoholic beverages, we may affect our nervous system.

The effects we stated for each case occur in the short-term. However, they may also have long term effects on the body. Case 1 may add weight to our body system if we do this on a regular basis, thereby affecting other systems in the body. Case 3 could impact the body system over long periods of time if the contamination is the wrong kind, possibly leading to death. Case 4 can have bad long term consequences, from increased weight gain and associated problems to destruction of some parts of other body systems including the nervous system, urinary system and reproductive system.

The important points in this section then tell us that a system can be complex and made up of many parts; a system has inputs, outputs and feedback mechanisms; and a system affects and can be affected by other systems outside of our system.

We will see that applying systems thinking to our body could significantly impact our current exercise, diet, activities, and habits.

A Model is More Than Just a Beautiful Face

In this book, a model is something we use to represent important parts of the real world. Models can be produced at almost any stage in thinking in Our Systems World. Our models are representations of the real thing (but not the real thing) and usually contain representations of only important parts of the real thing. The words **important parts** tells us that we should not try to put everything in our representation – only those items that are important to our current thinking and interactions in Our Systems World. These models (or representations of what is important in the specific case with which we are concerned) are often very useful in understanding a given situation in Our Systems World.

We can generate different representations or models of the same basic object depending on the context of our thinking. For example, we can think of a model of the human body in several different ways. One way which we have already modeled the human is via biological systems as discussed above such as the digestive system and the nervous system. This approach would be helpful in medical diagnosis and subsequent treatment of a disease.

A second approach would be to take parts of the body such as the:

- Head
- Torso
- Arms
- Legs
- Hands
- Feet

These concentrate on specific body parts where each part can contain many of the systems mentioned above (e.g., a hand contains parts of the skeletal system, muscular system, nervous system, and circulatory system). This model might be more important in repairing physical injuries such as a broken hand.

Another model of a human might look at the human system as a node in an information system. The human is both a source and a receiver of data, a processor, a storage device, and a communication link. We can further divide this model into sub-models such as a human data model and a human processor model.

We can continue to develop more models of the human as a part of a system, say in a manufacturing system (e.g., assembler) or a transportation system (e.g., driver, pilot).

So reiterating the important point, a model should represent only those items that are relevant to the systems thinking or analysis at hand.

How About Those Business Systems?

Businesses are structured in many different ways to try to optimize their operations in their specific marketplace. Whatever the structure, the elements within the organization and the external connections must work together in some way to keep the organization a viable entity. Each organization forms a system. An expanded system is formed as its external connections are added. This resulting system forms the organization's Systems World. Within an organization's Systems World, there are many possible forms or structures.

Environmental Representation - One organizational form emphasizes the organization's environments. Within the organization (called the internal environment), we can group the organization's elements such as people, facilities, products, policies and procedures, culture and unique ways of doing business. Outside the organization (the external environment) we find elements such as customers, suppliers, partners, competitors, government regulations, and trade associations. These must connect to the internal organization. By describing the internal and external connections among the environments – and – by describing each of the elements, we can get a good understanding of the organization and its operations. We can document this information using words, tables and/or visual representations. We will describe approaches for visually representing such a Systems World in more detail in Chapters 4 and 7.

Departmental Representation – We can also represent our organization's Systems World in terms of Departments. If you look at many organization charts, you may find departments represented with names such as Finance, Marketing, Research and Development, Design, Manufacturing, etc. These designations are what we often call functional elements, i.e., describing the functions that the departments perform. (I discuss functions in more detail in Part III). Each of these departments contains people, facilities, products, and links to both the inside and the outside world. These are also the environmental elements described above. Although we divided the organization into parts that are different than we did in the environmental representation, we are still describing the organization's Systems World.

Business Information Systems – An important element that is usually available within an organization (or contracted to an external organization) is a Business Information System. This system provides capabilities to collect, sort, manipulate and produce useful data and information. This product may be as simple as a spread sheet for doing your income taxes or a word processing system that helps you write letters and reports, or very complex such as transaction processing systems or management information systems. Regardless of their size, they follow the simple design shown in Figure 2-1 earlier in this chapter, i.e., Input, Processing System, Output and Feedback.

Therefore, an information system is a set of interconnected elements that collect (input), manipulate (process), and produce (output) data that is used to accomplish a goal or objective. Of course some systems are designed to be more focused on solving certain types of problems and processing needs. This makes them more efficient. We can use standard PCs in many cases as a general processing machine that can attack many different problems when using the proper software, but it is normally not optimized to solve one type of problem. Often more complex machines may be required to achieve better efficiency.

Never-the-less, our information system is part of our organization's Systems World.

The Human Element Strikes Again

As we work our way through the rest of the book, I emphasize one key point. Almost always the critical pieces of any system are the people involved in the system. People affect the design, use, and interface (getting the inputs and using the outputs). System after system has failed because of the incorrect use of the people involved. Failures rates in information systems design and use range up to 80%. No one really knows what the actual failure rate is, but it is a large number involving billions of dollars. In my career, I have been asked to review and recommend approaches to take an organization's information systems project from failure to success too many times.

In our definition of a system, we say that a system is a collection of elements (things) working together to reach some goal. In an information system, the "things" include people, procedures, processors, software, and data.

Even as we apply these concepts to individuals in their everyday lives, understanding the people, systems and environment are critical to solving problems and making good decisions. So in Our Systems World, we must be sensitive to the human element associated with the decisions and actions we are planning to take.

Fix it or Die

Another important idea is the concept of critical systems. There are systems or parts of systems that, even when broken, permits the system to continue to function, albeit less effectively. There are other systems or parts of systems that when broken forces the system to fail. Think of a wing on an aircraft or the human heart. If these parts of their system fail, the larger system fails (i.e., the aircraft and the human body). These systems are critical to the operation and are called critical systems or critical parts of a system. As we proceed further in this book, we will see that when we are trying to make decisions, we have to determine if there are any systems that are critical in making our decisions. If they aren't, these systems become secondary considerations. Hence, in some cases, it is important to think about many of these other factors; in other cases it is a waste of our time. So a part of systems thinking is to learn to determine what is important and what is not as we attempt to reach our goal.

CHAPTER 3

SYSTEMS THEORY vs. SYSTEMS THINKING

In the Beginning

Although the concept of systems has been around for a very long time, we only began to see a formal approach of thinking about systems emerge in the first half of the 20th century. During this time an approach to analyzing systems was developed called general systems theory.

General systems theory basically says that the best way to analyze a system is to divide the system into its parts (elements) and analyze these smaller pieces and their interconnections. This breaking down (dividing) the system and then analyzing the parts is called **systems analysis**.

Looking back at our earlier definition of a system, we said that a system is a bunch of elements that interact to achieve some goal. Therefore our definition is in agreement with the basic concept of systems theory. We further determine that general systems theory can apply to almost anything that has more than one element.

We can apply this same concept (breaking down a system into its parts, analyzing the parts, and putting them back together in a better way) to many different areas of interest. For example, we can apply this concept to solving many different types of problems and in helping us make better decisions. This is one of the key concepts in Our Systems World and will be used throughout this book!

As systems theory is applied to different problems, it becomes clear that one can gain a better understanding of how complex systems are structured and how they work. This leads us to the ability to reconstitute newly structured systems that contain less complex and more efficient parts than existed in the original system and which can help us accomplish the desired goal(s).

But wait! There is another way of looking at and analyzing systems. Instead of breaking a system down into its elements and interactions among the elements, suppose we look at the effects of actions performed both on the total system itself as well as on other systems connected to the original system. This approach is often called **systems thinking** and was first used extensively in the mid-to-late 1950s by Professor Jay Forrester of MIT to test out new ideas in societal systems.

Systems thinking looks at the big picture and works from there. This is like looking at the earth from outer space and seeing the parts we need to accomplish something and how these parts are linked together. This approach looks at how the part of the system that we are studying interacts with other parts of the system. We say we are taking a high-level view of the interactions occurring in our system. As we progress with our analysis, we often find more and more interactions within our system. We need to take these interactions into account as we proceed toward our accomplishing our goal.

Note, however, this approach is not really different than our earlier discussions about expanding our system's view to encompass a larger system. For example, remember that our Air Transportation System can become part of the larger system that we called the General Transportation System. This concept of systems thinking can also be applied to developing our Systems World.

Some might argue that the systems thinking and systems analysis approaches use different ideas and tools. I maintain that for most environments in which we normally deal, the distinction between the two approaches is not relevant. So throughout the remainder of this book, I will use the terms *systems thinking* interchangeably with *systems analysis*. I will specify one or the other only if there is a distinct need for clarity. If I refer specifically to the standard definition of systems thinking, I will call it *classical systems thinking*. Similarly I will refer to systems analysis as *classical systems analysis*. Later in this book I will present tools that we can use that allow us to develop Our Systems World, make decisions, and solve problems using both approaches.

Systems Thinking and Systems Shrinking

I call this section Systems Thinking and Systems Shrinking because I believe that these terms makes sense as we develop Our Systems World.

When we reduce the complexity of our system by breaking our system down into smaller and smaller pieces (in other words, perform our classical systems analysis), we are in fact shrinking the sizes of the pieces of our original system, hence the term systems shrinking.

When we do not reduce our system to its smaller pieces, but look at the system as a whole, I call our approach systems thinking.

Significant research and analyses have been performed over the years in both systems analysis and systems thinking. They have been applied to the design and development of many technical and societal systems and have been used to help make decisions and solve problems.

So applying the ideas of systems thinking to our needs is straight forward. We can think of systems thinking as nothing more than looking at interactions among the parts of our system from a systems perspective in Our Systems World.

Systems thinking can benefit the individual and the organization. Among the potential benefits if one adopts the Systems World perspective are:

- Better understanding of our environment
- Better problem solving and decision making
- Better communications and interactions with others
- Better planning and use of resources
- Better products
- Better ways of doing business

High Level, Top Down and Bottom Up

High-Level Analysis – This approach to solving problems, analyzing our systems, or understanding our environment in nothing more than our classical systems thinking approach discussed above.

Top Down Analysis –. When we talk about top down analysis we mean that we are looking at the environment, system or problem from its original starting point. In other words, for our system we are looking at the system and how it interacts with other systems. We then take our system and the break down our system into smaller and smaller pieces (in other words our classical systems analysis). Often these smaller pieces are called subsystems, but in fact they are systems themselves. We must not lose sight of the interconnections that exist among our systems and subsystems.

To illustrate the approach, let us look at our Air Transportation System again. If we analyzed the system by dividing it into the major subsystems such as the airplane, air traffic control system, etc., and perhaps further divided each of these subsystems into their own subsystems (sub-subsystems) such as the subsystem Airplane into the sub-subsystems propulsion, structure (wings, fuselage), etc., we would be performing the classical systems analysis approach. We then analyze the effect that the appropriate components have on our system. This top down approach applies to solving many problems and assisting in decision making.

Bottom Up Analysis – In our top down analysis, we broke our system into its elements (component parts). If, however, we started with a group of elements and then combined and interconnected them to build a larger system, we would be doing a bottom up analysis. We determine the key interactions among the separate systems and slowly build (or rebuild) our system using the parts that are relevant to our reaching our goal. This approach is often called systems engineering. Again it is often a part of our problem solving and decision making activities.

Summary – Which approach is the best one to use? It depends on what you are trying to do and what information you have when you start your analysis. If you start with a group of elements (say the elements within a business such as finance, marketing, engineering, manufacturing, distribution and so on), and you want to build a more efficient organization, some people will say to interconnect these to form the overall organization.

Maybe so, but it is often a better approach to do a top down analysis first to analyze the details of each of the business elements (e.g., finance, marketing) and to see where the different activities within each organizational element actually should interconnect. This could result in a significantly different organization than a bottom up approach would produce. As an example, in defining an information system for a corporation, as one breaks down the business functions that a corporation performs, one can more easily determine the key information functions and their interactions. This can lead to an effective and efficient system to solve the corporation's information needs. It further makes it easier to design, implement and test a new information system resulting in fewer problems and lower costs.

One can further argue that we really need to know how the organization interacts with or needs to interact with the outside world before we do anything else. I believe that this high level investigation is very important to the final design of the organization.

When possible, I often combine all three approaches: high-level, top down and bottom up in that order. The following steps illustrate one simple approach to restructuring an organization.

- First try to understand the problems to be solved, the goals that you want to reach and the environment in which you are operating
- Then try to understand what is needed in the system to achieve the goals identified
- Next begin to break the existing system (or problem) down into its elements
- Try to determine what is needed from the elements and different ways to combine and interconnect them
- Then recombine the elements into the new system (the solution)

As I go through each of these steps, I may use tools that are available to assist in making choices and decisions.

I will detail several of the steps and tools in more detail in later chapters in this book.

Feedback and Feed Forward

Another idea that we should think about as we start to evaluate and analyze our individual Systems World is the need to learn from our actions and the actions of others with which we interact. We might take some action and then we should evaluate the results of our action.

In certain physical systems the result might be very obvious. For example, if we crash our car into a tree, we can quickly determine the effects of the action: bodily injury to the car's driver and passengers, and physical destruction to the car. These results effectively feed back into our mind, telling us that if we crash a car into a tree bad things happen. Hopefully we learn from this example and *feed forward* this knowledge to the future so that if we later find ourselves in the position of designing the landscape for a roadway, we know we should minimize the chances that an injury can result from a crash. This may include keeping the maximum tree trunk diameter in a center aisle of a highway less than some specified size so that the tree would break with minimal impact on the car.

Other examples abound, even in your everyday activities. Think about it.

In the environment of societal systems, it is more difficult to determine cause and effect. For example, if we made inappropriate remarks about our superior at work and shortly thereafter we were reassigned to a less desirable job, perhaps there was some connection. Again, we may feel that we learned something from the feedback resulting from the original action.

I like to look at feedback and feed forward from the following perspective. What would happen if we took a certain action. The If… Then… approach helps us to better apply systems thinking to solve our problems and to make decisions.

It Has a Beginning, It Has an End

There is another important concept when we are talking systems – which in my case is most of the time. This concept is called the **Systems Life Cycle**. The systems life cycle describes what can happen or what has happened to a system from its birth to its demise. Let's take the human system as an example of a systems life cycle. A typical human is born, grows up learning new things, utilizes some of what is learned to exist through its mid life, grows old and dies. Some human systems have more inherent talent than others. Some human systems learn and apply more of what it has learned than others. Some human systems have accidents or contract diseases and die earlier than others. The combinations are nearly infinite, never-the-less, each human system has a systems life cycle.

The same principles apply to any other system. Our airplane is built, performs its stated objectives and wears out. Its life can be extended by improved maintenance, replacements of parts, or flying fewer trips. Again, the end eventually occurs. Businesses do the same thing. Studies have documented the birth and demise of corporate entities. Sometimes they are absorbed by other entities, and sometimes they just go out of business. Businesses often have to reinvent themselves to be able to continue to exist. This may require a different product mix, a change in management, a change in technology, and/or a change in finances. Of course, many other factors exist to help or hurt an organization. But it is critical as one does their systems thinking to make systems life cycle considerations one of their concerns.

A systems life cycle therefore is time dependent and fits nicely into our systems thinking approach. Things change over time. **Time, therefore, becomes a key factor in any analysis that we may perform.**

CHAPTER 4

WHAT ABOUT MY SYSTEMS WORLD?

My World, Your World, Our World

Everyone has their own Systems World. In My Systems World, I have connections to everything (and everybody) that affect me and connections to everything that I affect. We are connected to other people and they are connected to us. These connections may be direct connections such as to our friends, family, coworkers, and neighbors. These connections may be indirect connections such as the connections to people or other elements that we do not even know. An example of an indirect connection may occur when one uses pesticides on their lawn. These pesticides can get washed into streams during rainstorms and affect the quality of the water and the fish population. This pollution therefore affects our environment and the people connected to it.

Organizations can also have their own Systems World. In fact, any entity (any physical thing) can have its own Systems World. The entity may be a person or an object (for example, an airplane). Hence, any entity that can affect other entities has a Systems World.

Anything that we as individuals do can affect something else. We can affect, for example, other peoples' thoughts, actions, finances and/or well being. Our actions may cause a change in the physical environment, for example, the work environment changes if we install a new computer system at work. If each of us thinks about the possible effects that our past actions have had, we start to generate a picture of My Systems World.

Your coworkers and your family members each have their own Systems World. Parts of two individuals' Systems Worlds may overlap. In some cases the overlap is great, in other cases the overlap is small or nearly non existent.

There are two major ways to begin to understand My Systems World.

Venn Can Help Us Understand My Systems World

The first way to understand My Systems World is by using what are called Venn Diagrams. Venn diagrams are nothing more that a group of geometric figures that represent specific parts of My Systems World. These figures are often visually represented by ovals, but they can take on any shape. As an example of a possible Systems World, let's look at Figure 4-1.

Each of the areas represents a different part of My Systems World and many of them overlap. For example, we see that our workplace impacts our personal life, our finances, and our family life. If our workplace also affects our education, the business/workplace oval would also overlap the education oval.

As we delve deeper and deeper into each of these areas we get a better and better feel of what My Systems World looks like and the interconnections among and within the system parts. For example, we can decompose the Finances part into its components such as:

- Accounts Receivable
- Savings Accounts
- Checking Accounts
- Accounts payable
- Investments

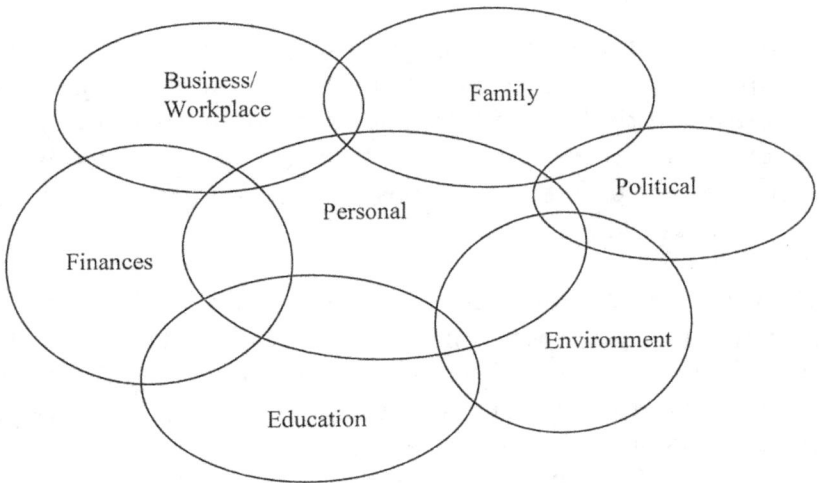

Figure 4-1 – My Systems World

We can then decompose the Investments part into:

- Stocks
- Bonds
- Real Estate

Next we can decompose the stock portfolio into mutual funds and individual stocks along with the number of shares and share price, dates purchased, dates sold, classification of stock (e.g., value), performance over time, and any other information that we need to make decisions.

We can further determine how our investments and their performance affect the other elements in Our Systems World. We can start to build the interconnections among the elements. Over time we need to continue to refine and update the interconnections as well as the data for each of the elements.

Sorry! This is not a one-time activity. As we continue to refine Our Systems World over time, it usually becomes easier to make certain decisions and, hopefully, much better decisions. In Chapter 6, I will present some additional ways to diagram (visualize) Our Systems World.

The approach of using Venn diagrams also works well in the business environment where the Personal space can be the organization (corporate enterprise) and the other ovals can represent the functional operations within the enterprise. In fact, this approach can help to determine where different functions should be in the organization based on the overlap of the diagrams.

What's Your Venn? – Take some time (if you can) to draw an initial Venn diagram for your own Systems World. Then add as much detail to each of your parts as you can. As you proceed through the book, add more details to your first Systems World diagram. Of course, your Venn diagram's details will change over time as you learn more and more about your Systems World. In addition, the next section can help you expand your understanding and diagramming of your Systems World.

Linked Nodes Can Help Us Understand My Systems World

A second approach to understanding My Systems World is to concentrate on the connections that we have with other entities in My Systems World. This is akin to the network interconnectivity of the internet. In technical speak, we are performing the analysis of the topology of networks of complex nodes.

Our approach is to determine what is connected together, why they are connected together and how they are connected together. The things that we connect together we call nodes or entities (the "parts" from our Venn diagrams). Each node has a given set of properties. Each individual, organization, and all other systems are nodes in a networked world. Each node is connected to one or more other nodes. Each node has properties associated with it. Each node is also made up of other nodes (often called sub nodes). This is the same concept as a system being made up of subsystems.

For example, in an information system, a node could be a computer (or group of computers). Each computer has certain characteristics associated with it. These characteristics can range from the speed of the computer to the size of its memory to the software that it has installed to the data that it has gathered. A node could also be a human being or an organization. An example of an organization node (enterprise node) and its connections are shown in Figure 4-2.

A node is connected to other nodes (linked) through some means of communications. The communications can take on many different forms. Some examples might be the communications through a wire or cable, through the air as radio signals, through a piece of paper that is carried from one node to another node, or through person-to-person contact. These details of the connections are important in determining the speed and costs of the communications.

We can deal with our nodes at different levels. Remember our Top Down analysis from the previous chapter. A top level view often gives us a good understanding of how the system is structured and possibly what it is trying to accomplish. This is part of our systems thinking initial approach to solving a problem or understanding an idea. The details of what goes on in a node may or may not be important in a given situation.

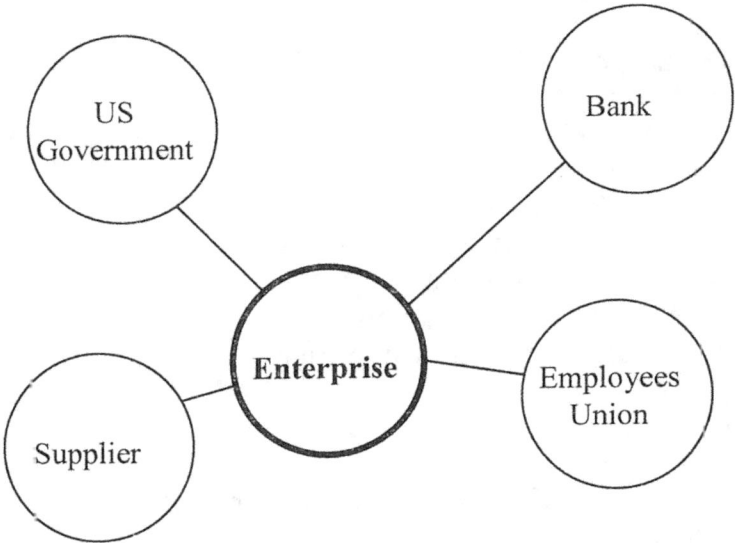

Figure 4-2 – Possible Top Level Linked Nodes for an Enterprise

What are the characteristics of the node that may be relevant to developing an enterprise's Systems World. Our enterprise is directly connected to other organizations. This level of detail gives us an overview of the key players, i.e., the key organizations that our enterprise has to deal with. Of course, as we add more detail, each node becomes more complex and more connections appear. There are software programs that can help us build our linked nodes as your network becomes more complex.

Let me expand the US Government node shown in Figure 4-2 to illustrate this point. Rather than drawing this expanded node, I am going to present the same information via a tiered list. Using lists could be a first step to drawing the linked node diagram. This list, shown below, contains the sub nodes found in the US Government node. I will further expand one of these sub nodes (the Department of Labor sub node) into its important sub nodes. It is sometimes easier to develop our nodes/sub nodes as a list, but it might not be as easy to understand this list as it would be to understand a picture or diagram.

Sub Nodes in the US Government Node

- Department of Labor
    - Wages
    - Health Plans and Benefits
    - Unemployment Insurance
    - Disability Resources
        - Americans with Disabilities Act
        - Employee Rights
        - Job Accommodation
    - Equal Employment Opportunity
    - Hiring
    - Labor Relations
    - Training
- Department of Health and Human Services
- Department of Treasury
- Department of Commerce
- Internal Revenue Service

This approach can be applied to analyze many different phenomena, including physical systems, social systems and biological systems.

What's Your Node? – What does your linked nodes look like? You should try to draw your high level nodes to begin to understand how to think using this concept in Your Systems World.

I Like Venns and Nodes

Both Venns and Nodes are useful tools in understanding Our Systems World. I suggest keeping new ideas and details of Venns and Nodes for important systems in a notebook or on your computer. Later we will learn to apply both Venn and Node techniques in developing My Systems World, solving problems and making decisions.

When Systems Worlds Collide

In Our Systems World we will come in contact with many individuals and groups. Some of these will have a profound effect on our thinking and actions. Other will have some reasonable amount of influence. And others will have little or no influence. This human side of Our Systems World is sometimes called our *Sphere of Influence*. The members in our sphere of influence may affect the way we look at things as well as our decision making.

Be aware that we may have individual, small group and company spheres of influence. Similarly, inputs into Our Systems World can come from the interactions of each of these spheres with the outside world. For example, our company's sphere of influence can be affected by market conditions, customers, competitors, governments, and weather. If the details in any sphere of influence changes, it can affect our thoughts, ideas, and actions. This is another example of how Our Systems World is constantly changing. A subset of our sphere of influence is the culture in which we operate. This is discussed briefly in the next section.

To Culture or Not to Culture? That is the Question

As we start to understand Our Systems World, it is important to determine the role that organizational culture plays in our world and in our decision making. By culture I mean the elements in our group environment and the beliefs in our group environment. Our cultural organization could be our family, neighborhood group, school, or business. Every group has rules or assumptions (often unstated) that the group expects everyone in the group to follow. For example, in a business everyone might be expected to work 5 extra hours per week without pay. Our home culture might expect us to interact with only certain groups of people.

In certain environments, going against the prevailing culture may be difficult and may affect our decisions. If this is the case then the culture should be taken into account as we analyze what and how we will react to different situations.

Our Systems World culture can therefore influence our thinking, our actions, our decisions, and the way we approach solving problems. We need to understand these effects and make a conscious decision whether they will influence us or not. It is often easier to go along with the crowd, but we need to know what we want to achieve before we let the crowd influence us. Further along in this book we will discuss how to generate our goals and how they can influence our actions and decisions.

So it is important to understand the influences in Our Systems World. If we understand these influences, we can factor them into our decision making to come up with the best decisions.

CHAPTER 5
CAN I MODIFY MY SYSTEMS WORLD?

I Think, Therefore I Can

So you really want to change your world.
You want to advance at work.
You want better relationships with other people.
You want to improve your financial conditions.
You want the good life.

If you are a company, you want to improve your business.
You want to increase your stock price.
You want to be recognized as a good place to work
You want to keep your employee turnover low.
You want to become more efficient and effective.
You want to increase your return on investment.
You want to keep your officers and stockholders happy.

Great! But are you really ready to do what is necessary to better understand Your Systems World? Are you willing to try to apply systems thinking to change and improve Your Systems World? Will you do your homework before you make decisions or solve problems? It takes time and effort to change the way you do things. But it is not impossible.

So far we have discussed the concept of My Systems World. We have begun to think about what we need to organize Our Systems World. We have introduced the concepts of systems thinking and systems analysis. We have started to lay the groundwork for what is needed to define and function in Our Systems World.

In Part II of this book, *Making Decisions in My Systems World*, we introduce the concept of making decisions and provide the tools to help you make good, better, best decisions that we can make with the information we have in hand and with our individual mind set, i.e., the way we make our decisions.

In Part III of this book, *Systems Thinking and Solving Problems in My Systems World*, we identify five steps we will need to better implement the systems thinking concepts that we are developing in this book.

So back to the question, Can I Modify My Systems World? Yes! Sure! Absolutely! Any entity (individual or corporation) can change. Change is inevitable, but the ways each entity changes can be extremely different. Among other things it depends on your risk tolerance.

What Kind of a Risk Taker Are You Anyway?

If we look up the term risk in a dictionary, it says something like this: "possibility of loss or injury." Let's apply that definition to what we do on an everyday basis. If we drive to work, what is the risk? Are we willing to take that risk? Why? Are the rewards worth it?

This risk/reward tradeoff is something that we are dealing with all the time. Often we consciously don't even consider the risk involved in our actions. Just think of all we do during a day that can impact our and other people's lives.

Other times, risk analysis is critical in our making decisions. Should we quit our job to go back to get a college degree? Think of the income that we are losing. Our circle of acquaintances might change. Have we picked the right subject? Can we do the work needed to get the degree? If we have a family, how will it impact them?

As a corporation, did the enterprise consider the disruption in operations by restructuring the way that it is doing business? Does the enterprise have the resources to implement the changes? Is there a plan in place to handle problems in the implementation? What are the real benefits derived through this new course of actions? What do the shareholders think? And so on.

The point of presenting these questions is to determine if we are ready to take different levels of risks to receive possible (unsubstantiated?) rewards. The answers to these and many more questions will help us determine if and how we may want to modify Our Systems World. And if we do, how might we manage the risks.

In the following chapters, I present techniques that can help us identify possible risks arising from making certain decisions.

OK – Tell Me Again Where We Are Headed

Let me take a little time to go over what we have accomplished up to this point. As I stated above, I want us to start to think differently about the world around us. To help us do this, we introduced the concept of My Systems World – that is, the world that belongs to only us. Our Systems World has things (elements) within it and contains links and connections to many people, places, things and ideas. All these things make up Our Systems World. We said that a system means a collection of elements that work together to achieve some goal. Our individual Systems World with all its interconnections tell us that each of our actions affect many other elements in Our Systems World, some strongly and some weakly, and that we should consider these outcomes as we think and do things.

Some of these outcomes can be extremely important, yet others might appear to be insignificant. "Appear to be" is an important phrase here because we often miss the connections to other elements when we do our thinking and analysis. In other words, we often lose sight of what we are trying to accomplish, i.e., the goal of the activity. This leads us to the concept of Systems Thinking which consists of several approaches to help us understand Our Systems World and the consequences of our actions.

Our Systems World can contain many complex systems within it – physical things and people and ideas. Our goal may be too difficult to achieve if we just attack it as is. We learned that we can look at our problem or system from different viewpoints, for example, from a top down perspective. We can break our system into smaller pieces, with each smaller piece easier to understand. Doing this can often help us in making our decisions. We can combine these results to help us attack the total problem and achieve our goal.

We also gained some ideas about how to view the relevant and important systems and elements through Venn and Node diagrams. This helps us get a better feeling for what we have, how to analyze each area, and how to understand the connections between the areas. We also identified other areas that we need to consider when deciding to do something, areas such as the good and bad risks we might encounter.

Just Follow the Yellow Brick Road

Unfortunately, we haven't learned many of the details needed to follow through on some of the above concepts and ideas. That is what we will do in the following chapters. When we want to fix something, it is usually good to have a set of tools available to use. In the next chapter we begin to introduce some of the tools that we need to make our job easier. These tools will include visualization tools to help understand what we will be seeing as we continue through this book.

We follow the chapter on visualization tools with chapters on techniques to use to help us make decisions and 5 steps needed to do Our Systems World decomposition. In other words, we will take what we have in Our Systems World, identify goals, divide our system into smaller pieces, and then put them back together better that they were before.

Hopefully when we are finished with this book, we will be using systems thinking in Our Systems World. To quote a TV personality: Better Ingredients - Better Pizza. If we use the ideas presented, hopefully we will produce better decisions.

CHAPTER 6
A PICTURE IS WORTH A WHOLE LOT OF WORDS

I Think I "See" Both the Problem and the Answer

Some people "see" pictures of what they are reading and hearing. In effect, they are visualizing the environment and the actions being described. This makes it easier to understand what is happening. This visualization also helps them plan actions they may take. They often mentally go through these possible actions step-by-step. But visualizing is not uncommon. How often when reading a novel do we visualize the physical environment, the characters in the story, and the action which occurs? Perhaps we have visualized how we are going to act in a meeting. Some actors visualize how they are going to play a part. Athletes such as a gymnasts, divers, skiers or dancers often visualize their routines before their performance. They "see" what each of their actions will be. This helps memorize and coordinate actions with timelines in their routines. These athletes therefore visualize their routines, producing detailed mental pictures of positions and actions they will take.

The same visualization techniques can be used to visualize the possible activities that may occur in My Systems World as we attempt to solve a problem or make a decision. We might see what can occur at a high level or at a detailed level.

We can expand this idea of visualization to include generating pictures, graphics or some other kind of visual representation of the situation under consideration. The old expression "A picture is worth a thousand words" often applies when we represent data in an easier to understand visual form. These visual representations of data or actions and activities can help us more easily interpret what is occurring in a particular situation. Better understanding of the environment and data can lead to better decision making.

In this chapter, I present some simple but powerful techniques to help us understand the problem we are trying to solve or the decision we are trying to make. Using these techniques can help improve our understanding of Our Systems World and help us develop a better solution or decision.

After reading this chapter, if we are interested in digging deeper into the use of visualization techniques, there is an excellent set of three books by Edward R. Tufte entitled *Visual Explanations, The Visual Display of Data*, and *Envisioning Information*.

I Hated Math in School - Just Show Me a Picture

One thing that many books try to do when talking about scientific concepts is to define the environment in terms of mathematics. In fact, using math can often simplify the definition of a problem and lead to a good solution. For those so inclined, using math is often easier than trying to figure out the right answer using intuition alone. There was a television police show called *Numbers* that tried to show how many of the activities in the real world can be described by mathematical theories. While this is true, when we are trying to solve many of the problems and make many of the decisions that we come across in our everyday activities, we often do not need the precision that a mathematical solution would give us. That is not to say that we should not use math at all in our analyses, but that we normally do not need detailed mathematical analyses.

Of course, there is another problem with presenting our ideas using complex mathematics. Most readers are not well enough versed in math and its complexities to be able to easily apply these mathematical approach to solve our problems. The techniques that I present are somewhat intuitive and can be applied rather simply with some practice.

In this chapter, I introduce some additional concepts for visualizing our environment beyond Venns and Nodes. If we train ourselves to use pictures, drawings, graphs and tables, then many of the concepts that we are using become more understandable.

Let's further build Our Systems World. We can make it as simple or as high-tech as we want it to be. All we need is a pencil, a pad of paper, and the right attitude. If we want, we could add a computer with an Internet connection to help search for additional data and information, and to manipulate, store, and retrieve our data.

So here are some basic visualization techniques that can be very helpful in making decisions and solving problems.

Visualize This

General - Visualization techniques help a person to see what is happening by using pictures, drawings, graphs, charts and other visualization elements. Since we have seen that many elements in Our Systems World are interconnected, it becomes most helpful when we can see those relationships. However, it becomes more and more difficult to see what our environment looks like as the complexity of the relationships increase and the number of connections (links) increase. As a simple example, let's show how 6 people all linked to each other might look (Figure 6-1).

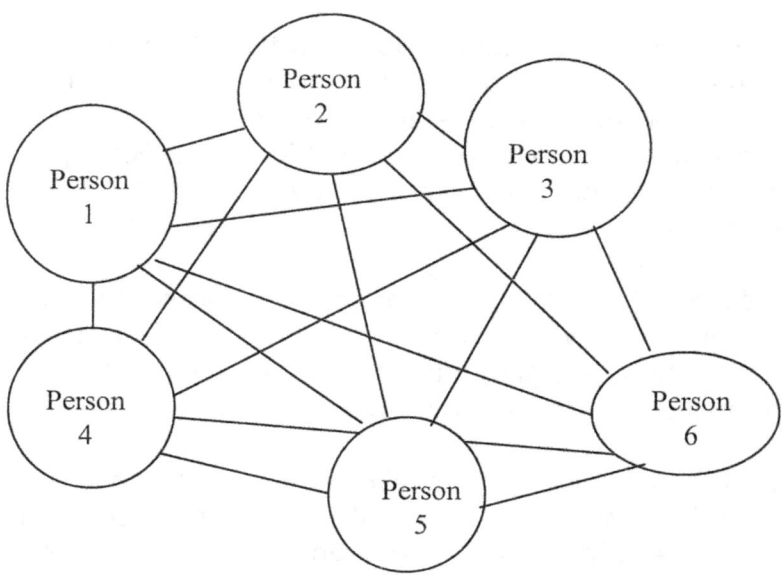

Figure 6-1 – Maximum Linkages Among Six Persons

We can count the number of interconnections from the diagram. This number is 15. As we get more nodes, however, we see that it becomes increasingly difficult to determine the maximum number of connections. We can describe the number of connections mathematically using the formula

(Number of Direct Connections) =
> (Number of persons) times (Number of persons less 1), all divided by 2

or

$$C = N(N-1)/2$$

So if we have 100 persons or elements in Our Systems World, we would have a maximum number of connections equal to C = (100)(99)/2 = 4950 connections if everyone was connected to each other. Of course normally not everyone is connected so the actual number will be less than 4950. However, an individual can have many more than 100 connections. So a change in a Systems World by one person can affect many other persons (elements).

Suppose not everyone in Figure 6-1 knew each other. This is shown in Figure 6-2 and assumes that no one knows more than three other persons.

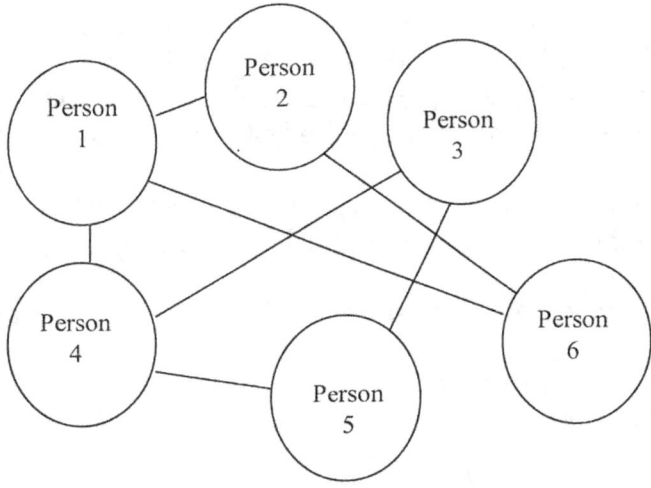

Figure 6-2 – Minimal Number of Linkages

We see that Person 1 is connected to all of the others, some directly and some through friends. In this case the number of connections is reduced to 7 from 15. This number can be further reduced to a minimum of 5 and still allow Person 1 to be connected to all the others, either directly or indirectly. Using the diagram may have made it easier to "see" the connections, as opposed to trying to describe these situations in words.

Dependency Diagrams - Another visualization technique uses linked elements called dependency diagrams. These diagrams show how things or actions we take are related. For example, if we order a blender from a catalog, a simple dependency diagram is shown in Figure 6-3.

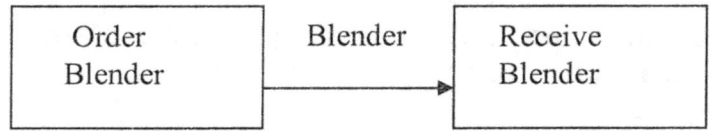

Figure 6-3 – A Dependency Diagram (Activity Diagram)

We cannot receive the blender until after we have ordered it, so "Receive Blender" is dependent on "Order Blender." On the line between the two boxes, we see the word Blender. This means that the item "Blender" is moved from the first to the second box.

The boxes in this figure show actions (or activities) occurring. The line connecting the boxes show a physical thing (entity).

We will use two types of dependency diagrams. They are called:

1.   Activity Diagrams, and
2.   System Diagrams.

They both look the same and only differ in what we are dealing with – activities or physical things (systems).

In activity diagrams we see that activities are nothing more than the actions that someone might take. An easy way to remember what we mean by an action is that an action usually starts with a verb, e.g., "identify product" or "collect data" or "read and analyze reports." Hence, our example in Figure 6-3 is an activity diagram. [Note: our activities are called "functions" by some researchers, and what we are doing is called functional analysis. Also from a data perspective, these diagrams are often called data flow diagrams.]

Systems diagrams often deal with physical things, for example, airplane parts. These diagrams also apply to data or to business systems. Figure 6-4 is a systems diagram.

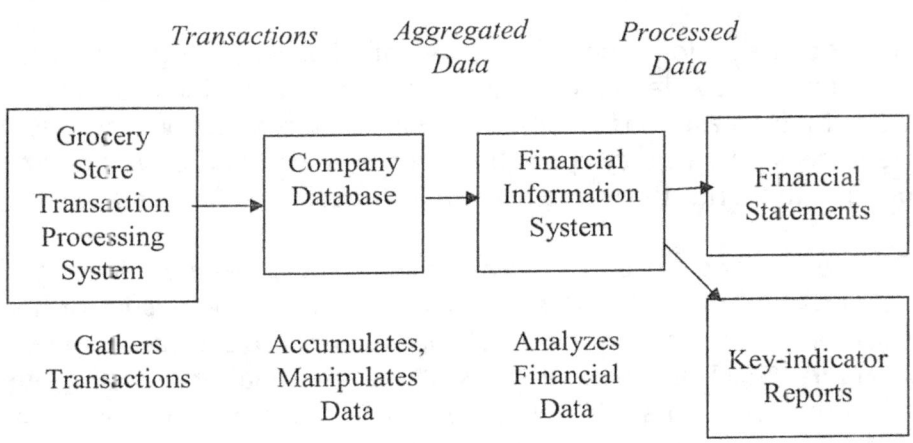

Figure 6-4 – A Dependency Diagram (Also called a Systems Diagram)

Each of the boxes is a physical thing (system or data). We can get fancy and draw one type of box for our data and a different type for our system, but it is not really necessary in our typical Systems World.

The important point here is that we draw what we think is happening in our world, i.e., we are visualizing the problem or situation. Then we can modify the diagram(s) as we learn more or as things change.

Loop Diagrams – A loop diagram allows us to explore the interrelations among elements in Our Systems World from a different perspective, one that expands on our idea of feedback which we discussed in Chapter 3. A loop diagram starts at one point in time and builds on the activities that occur. At some point in time it connects back (i.e., feeds back) into an earlier part of the loop.

There are at least two types of loops that occur when we are discussing feedback loops. The first type is called a reinforcing loop that provides positive feedback to our system. This means that if something in the loop changes, then another element in the loop changes in the same way. For example, if we increase the amount of food we feed our pet, the pet's weight will increase.

The second major type of loop is called a balancing loop that provides negative feedback. In this case if something increases in the loop, this increase causes something else to decrease. For example, if we increase the money spent from our Research and Development budget, the funds that remain in our R&D account will decrease.

The speed and magnitude of positive and negative feedback depends on both the nodes involved and the characteristics of the links connecting them. An example of a causal loop diagram is shown in Figure 6-5. This example looks at the interrelations among our elements when a manufacturing company is determining how much of its funds to spend on research and development.

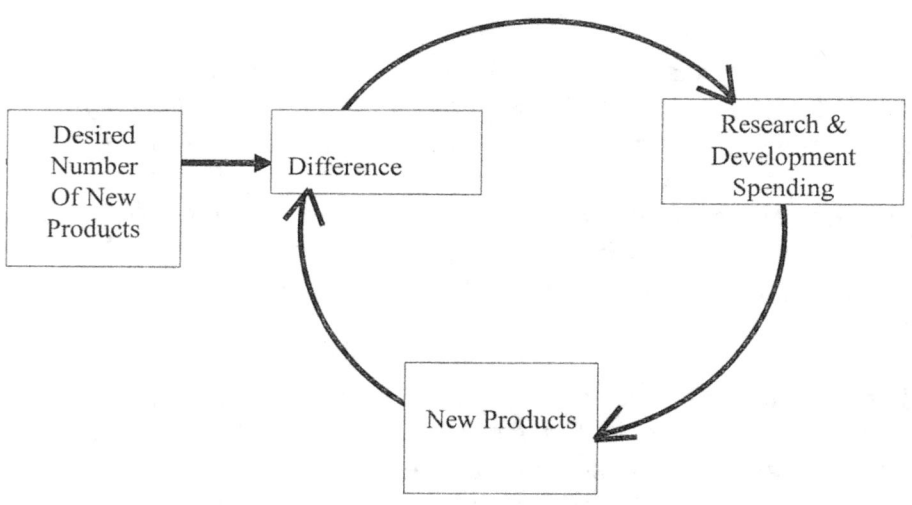

Figure 6-5 – Loop Diagram

From Figure 6-5 we see that the loop from "Difference" to "R&D Spending" is a reinforcing loop (positive feedback) since if the difference between what we want verses what we have in the way of new products is positive, then we need to increase our R&D, and if it is negative we need to decrease our R&D. Similarly, if our R&D goes up, we should increase the number of new products we develop, hence another reinforcing loop.

Assuming we started out with the need for several new products, if we increase the number of new products, then we will reduce the difference between what we want and what we have, hence here we have a balancing loop (negative feedback). So Figure 6-5 has two reinforcing loops and one balancing loop.

 Just a few hints on developing your loop diagrams: (1) the elements should be nouns or noun phrases, (2) think about how one element affects not only the next element, but elements further around the loop, and (3) we can have complex loops and multiple loops that interconnect.

Graphing - We use graphs all the time in newspapers, TV and magazines as well as in the stock market and corporate financial reports. Graphs are a visual presentation to allow comparisons among various situations. As an example, suppose that we want to see what happened to our income and outflow of our money over the last several months. One way to visually see this is via a graph. Of course we can make a list and look at our finances that way, but visual presentations often make it easier to do comparisons. Our finances might look like Figure 6-6..

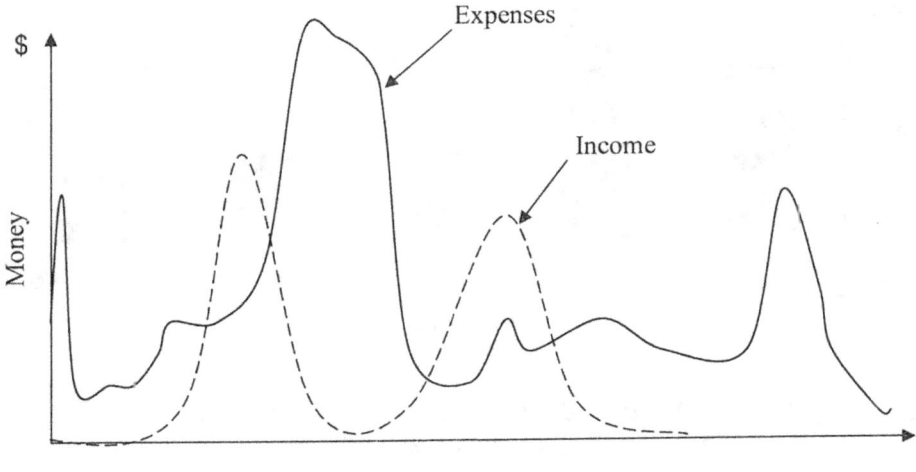

Figure 6-6 – Finances over Time

If this is our income verses expense curve, we probably are having financial difficulties since the expense curve is quite a bit greater than our income curve. It is easy to see what is happening by looking at the curve. In this case, looking at the areas under each of the two curves and comparing them is a good indication of our financial condition. If we could measure the areas, we would get a good approximation of the actual dollar differences between our income and expenses.

Bar Charts – Other graph types commonly in many areas to display data are bar charts and pie charts. Bar charts are often used in financial time-to-time comparisons. Bar charts can be either horizontal or vertical, and can get quite complicated. For example, in Figure 6-7, we see a vertical bar chart. This chart shows that there are 33 (8 + 14 + 4 + 4 + 3) models of hybrid vehicles and that 14 are in the $25,000 to $35,000 price range.

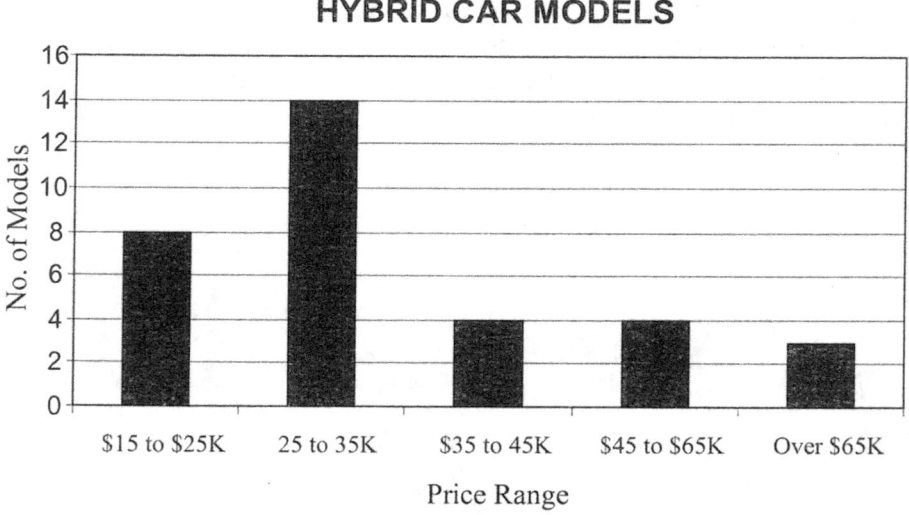

Figure 6-7 – Vertical Bar Chart Showing Number of Hybrid Car Models Available

In Figure 6-8 we see a horizontal bar chart. This chart describes the number of US immigrants from a given region in the world for selected years between 1900 and 1990.

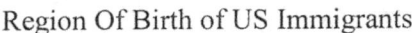

Region Of Birth of US Immigrants

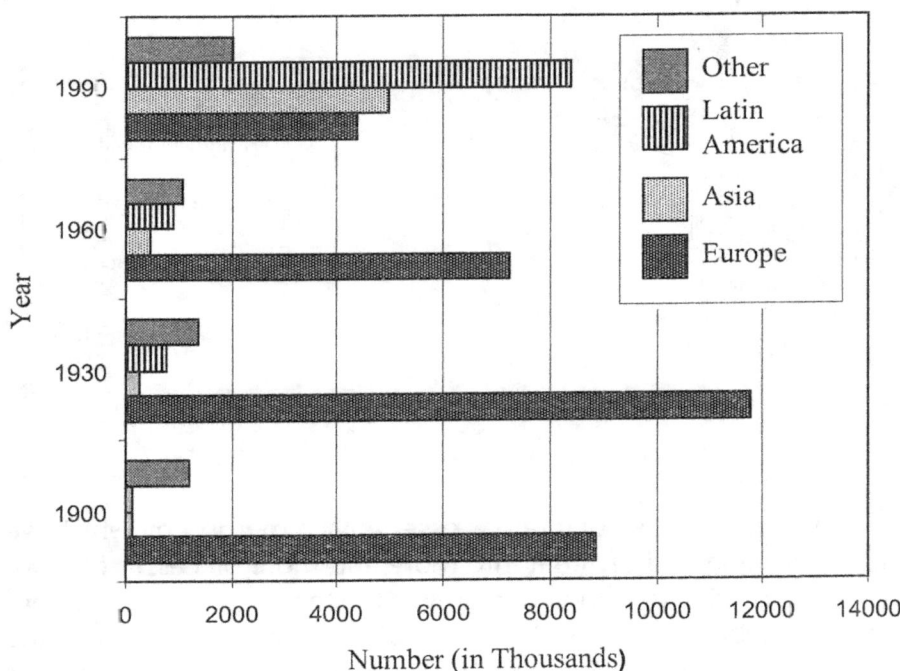

Figure 6-8 – Horizontal Bar Chart

Pie Charts - Another useful graph is the pie chart. These usually indicate the amount of any element compared to the rest of the individual elements. An example is given in Figure 6-9 that shows a sample mutual fund portfolio as a function of the types of holdings in that portfolio. Percentages of each category can also be added to this chart if so desired.

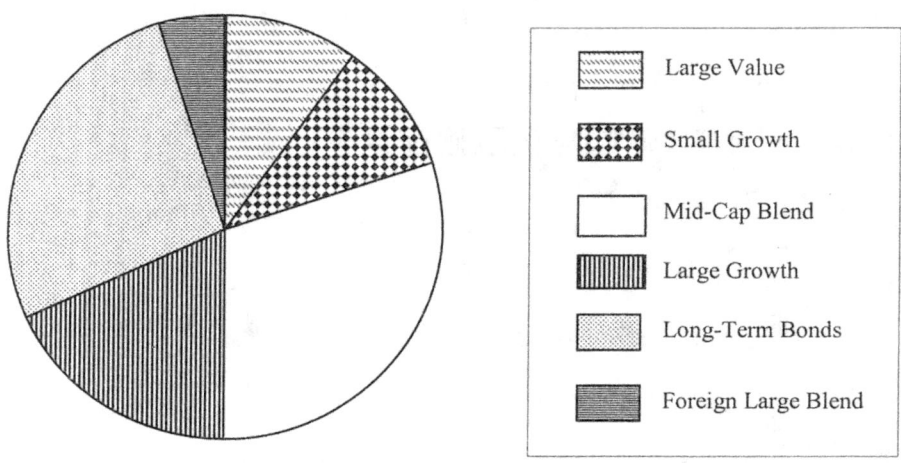

Figure 6-9 – Sample Mutual Fund Portfolio

Tree Diagram - A tree diagram is essentially a method by which we take something and divide it into more and more pieces. In fact, we are decomposing the original element (system) into its component parts. Going back to our airplane example, we can divide the airplane into pieces as shown in Figure 6-10. [Note: this airplane description is not complete.]

We can continue this decomposition of the airplane, but notice that it looks like an upside down tree; hence it is called a tree structure. The arrowed lines are the branches and the box named "airplane" is called the root. We can build our tree top-down or bottom up as we discussed in an earlier chapter.

Tree diagrams are very important in many of our analyses and decision making activities. For example, corporate organization charts are often presented as tree diagrams. We will discuss trees in more detail in Part II.

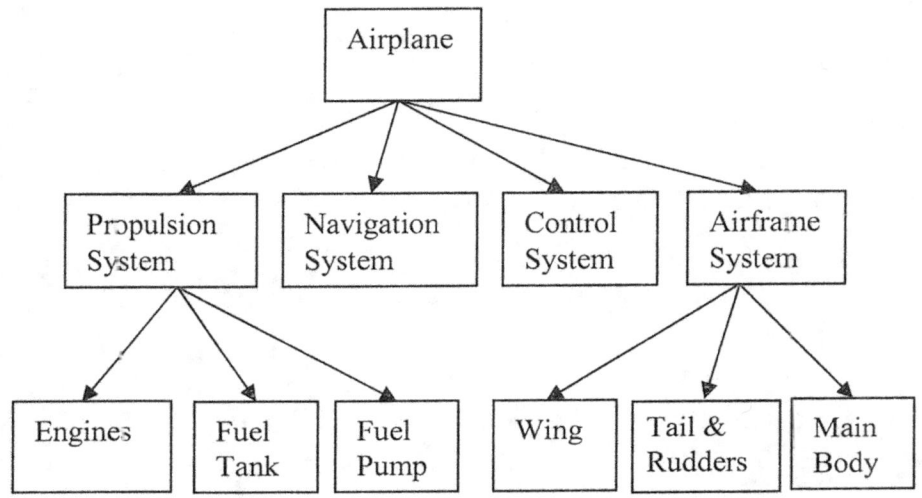

Figure 6-10 – Airplane Tree Diagram

PART II
—
MAKING DECISIONS
IN
MY SYSTEMS WORLD

CHAPTER 7

DECISIONS! DECISIONS! WHAT'S A PERSON TO DO?

One Approach for You, Another Approach for Me

Your Systems World is constantly changing. In fact, it changes every time you make a decision and take action. When each of us makes a decision, we choose one alternative from a set of alternatives. But to make the best decision, there is more than just making the choice. There is the preparation that is needed to get to that place where we can make the choice while having the best information that we can get under time and expense restrictions. We need to identify what we are trying to accomplish, come up with a set of good alternatives, make our decision and put the decision into action. The techniques for doing this are given in Part III of this book.

For now, let us try to get a good understanding of decision making and the tools that we can use to make those decisions. We see that we need to make decisions about both the solving of problems and the identifying of opportunities. For example, we might need to determine how to reduce the business losses of a particular division in our organization. Or possibly, we might need to determine which job offer we should take from the three that we have received.

Making decisions is not always an easy thing to do, and making the "right" decision can prove to be mind boggling. Part of the problem is that we do not usually know what the right decision is. Things are often changing with time and we might not take all these changes into consideration when we make a decision. Furthermore, we have seen in earlier chapters in this book that we each have many, many links to other elements in Our Systems World, so taking a particular action based upon a decision we make can affect many other elements in Our Systems World. A problem for us is that we often do not know if we have made the right decision until some time in the future, be it days, weeks or years.

Is there something we can do to help us make better decisions? Of course! Applying systems thinking can help to frame the important possibilities and alternatives that we can select. Part III identifies and discusses 5 steps that we can take to help us make better decisions. The level of detail that we use in Part III needs to be tempered by the complexity of the decision that we are trying to make.

Many decisions that we as individuals make every day affect Our Systems World in a non-threatening way (e.g., where to eat lunch, etc.). *Wait a second. Our diet can affect your health both in the short term and the long term which in effect will affect other elements of Our Systems World.*

If a decision is important, even life threatening, then we must do the best we can. This often depends on the amount of time that we have to make our decision and our inherent knowledge of the subject areas. Very quick or instantaneous decisions must, by necessity, be made with little formal analysis. Gut reactions are often used to make decisions when there is little or no time to weigh arguments or perform mathematical analyses of every outcome, but instincts often reflect one's background and knowledge. Some decision makers use their instincts as the driving force behind their decisions. Others perform careful analyses to reach their decisions.

We often make snap judgments or impulse decisions. We see something we like and buy it. Sometimes it turns out to be the right thing to do, but more often than not, and if we are honest with ourselves, we probably shouldn't have bought it. Buyer's remorse strikes again. We also make snap judgments in other situations (e.g., at work, in social situations, in financial investing). This is our subconscious making decisions for us. Try to suppress these feelings and use conscious thought that uses more structured decision making approaches when possible.

Many factors come into play in making decisions.

- Wants verses needs
- Rewards versus risks
- Feelings verses knowledge
- Varied interactions with other persons and things (i.e., My Systems World)

We can use some of these concepts to refine our decisions after we apply more structured techniques.

What's Good for the Goose is Good for the Gander

In business, the Enterprise's Systems World is much greater in size and scope than that for an individual. The consequences of decisions also may be significantly different in scope and complexity. If we can't make the right decisions and correctly execute our decisions, the organization can be severely impacted. Studies have shown that the best organizations make good decisions and execute them quickly and effectively. Major strategic decisions such as what products to make, which markets to enter or exit, and how to allocate capital resources such as funds or personnel are critical to the organization's success.

The enterprise decision space, as it is sometimes called, is very complex. The amounts of interactions that will be affected by a corporate decision are tremendous, frequently requiring using formal decision making procedures.

Yet, even if an individual or an enterprise performs a thorough analysis of the problem, this does not guarantee that we have made the best choice. Never-the-less, a thorough analysis will most likely help us focus in on what we want to accomplish. So in this Part II, I discuss decision making approaches and provide a set of tools that we can use to make decisions. In Part III, *Systems Thinking & Problem Solving in My Systems World,* I present a 5 step approach to problem solving using our Systems Thinking ideas. To do a thorough analysis, we should follow the steps presented in Part III. Then when we need to make a decision, we can use the decision making concepts from this Part II.

Given that we have or can get the information that we need to help us make the right decision, we can usually achieve, if not the optimal results, at least ones that are acceptable – i.e., ones that are good enough.

If we train ourselves in decision making concepts, therefore, we should be better prepared to make better decisions. This is why our firefighters, military, etc., train and train so that decisions can be made under time limited and stressful conditions.

To Err is Human, To Forgive Devine

Since essentially every action we take requires us to make a decision, and since every decision we make has an effect on Our Systems World, we want to do the best that we can do. The decision we make might yield a success or a failure in meeting our goals. We want to increase success and minimize failure. Therefore, learning to make good decisions is a critical skill that everyone should master. The basics to making good decisions are not difficult. The difficulty arises as the complexity of the decision environment increases.

For example, if we are professionals trying to determine whether we should quit our existing job and go to work for another organization, we will need to gather relevant information about the impact to Our Systems World such as working conditions, effects on our personal and family life, possibilities for advancement, financial impact, travel requirements, etc. I present ideas to help us gather and use this type of information in the next Part of the book.

Similarly, if we are corporate executives and we are trying to determine how to make our enterprise more efficient and effective, our analysis becomes much more complex. The number of factors that we need to consider and the sheer magnitude of the data we need to analyze can be overwhelming unless we employ some rigorous techniques. We will be making many more decisions than the professional employee in the previous example. So we see that this case is a matter of magnitude and complexity. I also present information in the next Part of the book to help us get a better understanding of our environment and to build our Enterprise's Systems World.

Many recent decision makers have employed mathematical and statistical techniques, logical thinking, and societal concepts such as group consensus. Some researchers are looking at the functioning of the brain for clues to help in making decisions. Corporations may employ concepts such as scenario planning (looking at what might happen when other events happen) and data mining (basically letting computers analyze loads of data looking for patterns in the data that helps us decide what we should do). Organizations have also built computer based systems called executive information systems and decision-support systems, both designed to help support decision makers.

Never-the-less, the same general systems thinking applies in all cases.

Thinking Managers – Not an Oxymoron

Making decisions is what managers are supposed to do. It is what they are getting paid for. But different levels of management, on the average, often make decisions differently using different criteria. As one proceeds up the corporate ladder, the focus changes and the methods used need to be compatible with their new focus. Those that change in the right direction more quickly often move through the organization more quickly. Of course, we are talking averages here and one's advancement through an organization depends on many additional factors. Never-the-less, if we start to use systems thinking, this may help determine what changes are needed to move upwards.

There have been many studies by many reputable organizations that address this topic. I refer to one of these studies because it captures several key ideas that we need to think about as we examine how we will make our decisions in the future.

In a February 2006 article published in the Harvard Business Review entitled *The Seasoned Executive's Decision-Making Style* by K. Brousseau, M. Driver, G. Hourihan, and R. Larsson, the authors looked at two factors.

The first factor identifies the amount of information that a person uses to make a decision. One decision maker may require lots of data before making a decision. This approach may yield the "best" decision, but often it takes a lot of time and effort. A second decision maker just wants the key facts (i.e., a limited set of data), before a decision is made and implemented. This approach may require additional changes and testing as the decision activities are implemented.

The second factor used by the authors is the number of possible options that are tried in implementing the decision made. A decision maker may select one course of action, and plans to make things come out as he believes that they should. A second decision maker may generate a list of possible options and pursue multiple approaches, allowing for changes to the outcomes.

I have illustrated these 4 cases in Figure 7-1.

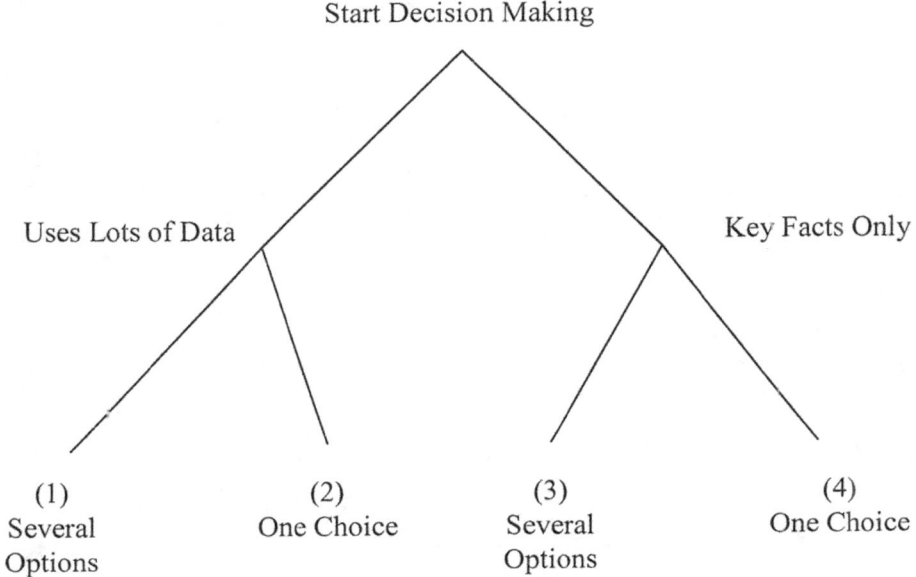

Figure 7-1 – Four Decision Making Approaches

These studies have shown that managers change their approach as the move up the management ladder. Top executives tend toward path (1) or path (2) above. Path (4) which combines the use of minimal information and a single option is dominant among first-level supervisors but nearly non-existent among senior executives. It is important for us to understand our approach to decision making based on our experience and temperament, what we want to accomplish, how this approach falls into Our Systems World, and to determine if we want to or need to change our approach.

CHAPTER 8

DECISION TOOL TIME

A Little Help Goes a Long Way – Using Decision-Making Tools

In the previous chapter, we introduced several ideas to get us prepared to make good decisions. Now we introduce a set of tools that we can use to assist us in making good, better, best decisions. There has been a lot of research in corporations and universities in developing decision making tools. I have selected a few of these that I believe are of particular use to the decision maker and do not require significant mathematics to effectively use. Once we learn these tools, then whenever we reach a decision point in Our Systems World, we can consider using them to assist us in making the decision.

Also as we go through Part III, which gives us step by step procedures to analyze problems and make decisions in Our Systems World, we will reach decision points where these decision concepts and tools can help us make the right decision.

It's Easy and Effective

As I mentioned earlier, we usually have to gather data to help us make our decisions and solve our problems. I go over data gathering in more detail in Part III. Suffice it to say that we need to be selective on which data we are gathering. We should try to get what we need but not much more. Of course, we will not always know what we need and will often gather too much useless data and miss some data we need. We can go back and gather new data if needed. Similarly, when we do our decision analysis, we need to identify those areas that we believe are important to our decision. It may turn out that some data that we are using is much more important to us than others that we are using. If this is the case we may want to "weight" some data as more important. We see this below in our simple (un-weighted) vs. weighted decision techniques.

Knowledge and data that we need is usually dispersed. We can gather data from sources such as the web, reports and books, our own files and knowledge, and groups of people. Human interaction data gathering can take on many forms such as "brain-storming" and "multi-voting" approaches where the members of a group suggest and discuss the possible data and its importance. Pooling of wisdom can be useful if correctly used. Many groups are often formed at all levels in Our Systems World. We can have corporate boards, committees, product development groups, management teams, or just an informal group (e.g., just sitting around a table or formed on-line). Group dynamics can come into play which can provide poor decisions – remember the old statement that a camel is a horse designed by a committee

I have selected eight techniques that can help us make our decisions. After reviewing each of them, I will discuss when we might want to use one technique over another. These eight techniques are:

- Pro/Con Analysis
  - o Simple
  - o Weighted (a.k.a. Force Field Analysis)
- Decision Tables
  - o Simple
  - o Weighted (a.k.a. Decision Matrix)
- Decision Trees
  - o Normal
  - o Weighted
- Pareto Analysis
- Clustering

Pro/Con Analysis

Simple Pro/Con Analysis - If we arrive at the point where our decision requires a selection of one of two choices (e.g., Yes/No, or item #1 vs. item #2), then one of the simplest ways to make decisions once we have done our homework is to make a simple Pro/Con list and see which appears to be the winner. As an example, for our next computer purchase should we buy a PC or a Mac computer? A Pro/Con list might look like the one shown in Figure 8-1.

BUY THE MAC?

PRO	CON
Better media capability	Costs higher than PC
Operating Systems Software Solid	More Software available on PC
Sleek Look	Fewer people have them
All components integrated into display unit	Only one company makes Macs
Takes less desk space	Must learn a new Operating System
Easy to connect my iPod and other components that I have	

Figure 8-1 – A Simple Pro/Con Analysis Table

Now you make a decision based on these Pros and Cons.

Weighted Pro/Con Analysis (Force Field Analysis) – A weighted Pro/Con analysis is also called a force field analysis. In this case the important elements are given more influence in the decision than those that are less important. Taking our example above, we can weight each element with a value of 1 through 5 where 1 is not important and 5 is very important. Doing that, we might get the table in Figure 8-2.

BUY THE MAC?

Wt.	PRO	CON	Wt.
4	Better media capability	Costs higher than PC	5
3	Operating Systems Software Solid	More Software available on PC	3
3	Sleek Look	Fewer people have them	2
1	All components integrated into display unit	Only one company makes Macs	3
1	Takes less desk space	Must learn a new Operating System	3
3	Easy to connect my iPod and other components that I have		
15	TOTAL	TOTAL	16

Figure 8-2 – A Weighted Pro/Con Analysis Table

Based on this analysis, we would choose not to buy the Mac computer. Since the totals are close, and if someone else weights the elements differently, then the decision might be different. For example, if cost is not important, but media capability is very important, then the decision will change to "Buy The Mac."

Note that you might see a force field analysis that looks very different than the table above although the results will be the same. The pros are often called the *forces for change* and the cons are called the *forces against change*. Each pro is shown in an arrow from the left towards the center and the cons in individual arrows from the right to the center. For example, see Figure 8-3 which is a subset of the example in Figure 8-2.

Decision Tables

Simple Decision Table - Another way to make decisions is with the use of decision tables. A simple decision table prioritizes a list of options. It is similar to our Weighted Pro/Con analysis, but with multiple options. However in this example, we are weighting each college on how it best meets our criteria in Our Systems World. Each factor, however, is NOT weighted in its importance to the other criteria.

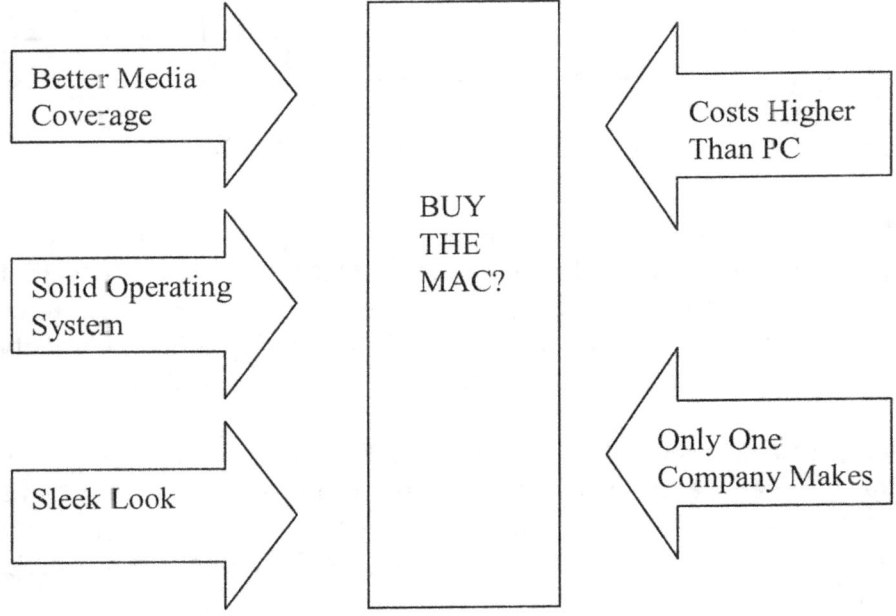

Figure 8-3 – A Force Field Diagram

The decision table in Figure 8-4 shows the selection of a college from a set of four possible colleges for the criteria that we feel is important to us. For this example we use the following weights.

- 4 = excellent match (to my needs and abilities)
- 3 = very good match
- 2 = good match
- 1 = somewhat of a match
- 0 = no match

FACTORS	College #1	College #2	College #3	College #4
Affordability of College	4	1 (very expensive)	2	3
Curriculum	3	3	2	4
Location of College	2	1	2	2
Social Life	3	2	2	3
Sports	1	2	3	3
Friends Attending	4	0	0	2
Quality of Food	2	3	2	2
Size of College	2	3	3	3
TOTAL	21	15	16	22

Figure 8-4 – A Simple Decision Table

This decision table says that College #1 or College #4 is the best match for our needs. Perhaps there are other factors of importance that we did not initially list (e.g., quality of research services, on-campus computer network, remote class attendance, quality of library, quality of instructors) which we could add to make a final decision.

Weighted Decision Table (Decision Matrix) – If, in the above example, each factor has a different importance to us in Our Systems World, then we can add weights to each factor as we did in our weighted Pro/Con analysis. We add weights to the individual factors as follows:

- 5 = Extremely important
- 4 = Very important
- 3 = Moderately Important
- 2 = Somewhat Important
- 1 = Not Important

Our example above then becomes the decision matrix shown in Figure 8-5. In this table, we just multiply the two weights (factor weight and college weight) to get the total weight.

Wt	FACTORS	College #1	College #2	College #3	College #4
5	Affordability of College	4x5=20	1x5=5	2x5=10	3x5=15
5	Curriculum	3x5=15	3x5=15	2x5=10	4x5=20
2	Location of College	2x2=4	1x2=2	2x2=4	2x2=4
3	Social Life	3x3=9	2x3=6	2x3=6	3x3=9
4	Sports	1x4=4	2x4=8	3x4=12	3x4=12
2	Friends Attending	4x2=8	0	0	2x2=4
1	Quality of Food	2x1=2	3x1=3	2x1=2	2x1=2
2	Size of College	2x2=4	3x2=6	3x2=6	3x2=6
	TOTAL	66	45	50	73

Figure 8-5 – A Weighted Decision Table (Decision Matrix)

In this example the order did not change, but the spread increased pointing to College #4 as the best choice.

A weighted decision table is useful for evaluating how to improve services provided by an organization, for example, the best way to improve Product Service Centers and Call Centers as well as improving operations of other types of organizations.

Decision Trees

Simple Decision Trees – In Chapter 6 (Figure 6-10) we presented a tree diagram of an airplane. We can use a tree diagram to help us make decisions. A tree diagram used in the decision making process is called a decision tree and takes the form shown in Figure 6-10, except that we make a decision at each node in the tree. A decision tree is often used to help determine the best path to take to reach a decision when the future environment is not certain.

A simple decision tree can be used to determine the various choices that we need to consider. In a simple decision tree we do not weight the importance of each path that we take. As an example of a Simple Decision Tree, let us look at the following problem.

<u>Problem</u> – (a) Should we centralize or distribute our Information Systems' capabilities, and (b) should we do it in-house or outsource the work when cost is a major factor?

<u>Solution Approach</u> - Our tree is shown in Figure 8-6 where the decision points are given by the circles with the "D" in them.

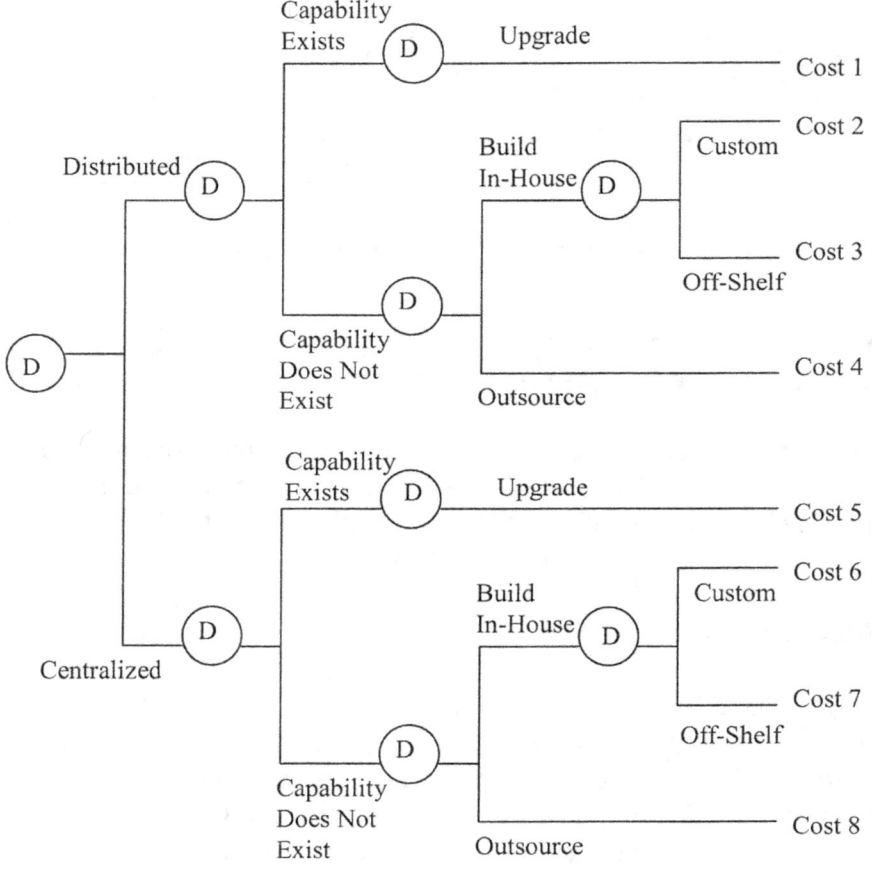

Figure 8-6 – A Decision Tree

This diagram is a simple description of the real world situation. I have not included several important factors such as security risk to corporate data when outsourcing to other organizations. The organization's Systems World could select a tree different based on the organization's needs.

Never-the-less, now that we have set up the tree, we can make decisions about each branch and eliminate those we don't need (called pruning the tree), finally arriving at the path(s) through the tree that we might want. A final step will be to calculate the costs of the branches that are left in our tree. Our tree has helped us concentrate only on the cost analyses of interest.

Weighted Decision Tree – A weighted decision tree will look similar to our simple tree above with the major difference being the addition of weights to our decisions. Many cases that use a weighted decision tree are attempting to determine the financial pros and cons of the different strategies, i.e., the different branches on the tree. The weights are given as the probability that the branch will be successful. The weights must add to 1 for each major branch in the tree. I will illustrate this shortly. We will generate numbers indicating the amount of money that the actions of a major branch might produce – and the highest income wins.

For our example, suppose that we have to determine which of two research projects we should continue to fund to produce a product that will provide the organization with the best possible return on the investment. In the marketplace, the product would be (a) successful, (b) moderately successful or (c) not successful. The probabilities for each of these 3 categories for a given product are determined by experts in the field. In some cases, we as individuals are the experts, especially for areas that are simple or those in which we are well versed. Let's assume our experts gave us the following information.

- Product 1 (major tree branch #1) is estimated to produce:
    o a profit of $800,000 with a probability of 0.25
    o a profit of $60,000 with a probability of 0.10
    o a loss of $80,000 with a probability of 0.65.

- Product 2 (major tree branch #2) is estimated to produce:
    o a profit of $300,000 with a probability of 0.65
    o a loss of $120,000 with a probability of 0.25
    o a loss of $20,000 with a probability of 0.10.

The decision tree is given in Figure 8-7.

EXPECTED VALUE

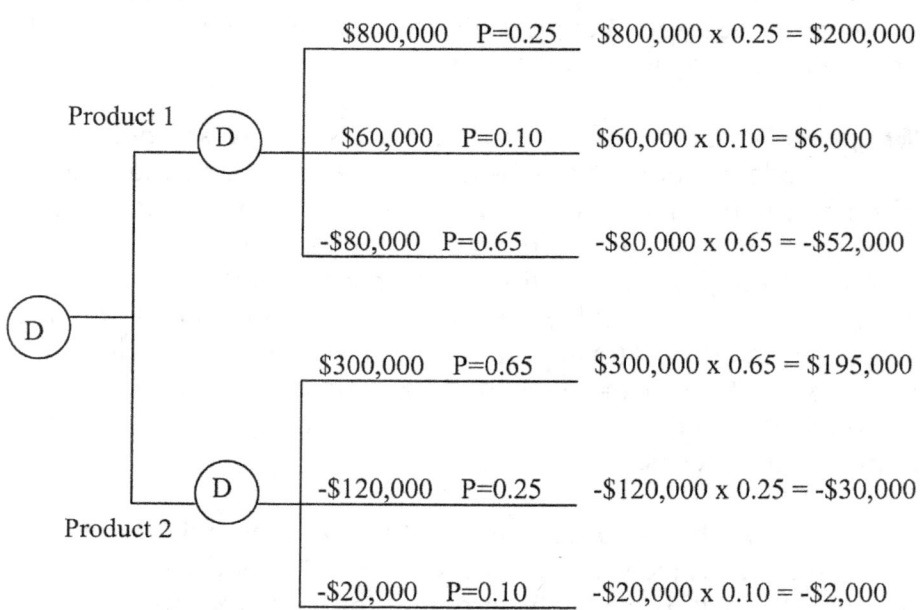

Figure 8-7 – A Weighted Decision Tree

We then perform the following steps to try to get a decision.

Step 1 - We first calculate the expected value of each branch by multiplying the estimated profit or loss by its probability.

Step 2 - We then combine the expected value for each Product by adding the expected values as follows.

- TOTAL EXPECTED VALUE OF PRODUCT 1 = $200,000 + $6,000 - $52,000 = $154,000

- TOTAL EXPECTED VALUE OF PRODUCT 2 = $195,000 - $30,000 - $2,000 = $163,000

This results in a decision that Product 2 provides the best expected value for our research dollars since Product 1 yields an expected value of $154,000 which is less than the expected value of Product 2 at $163,000. By taking the expected value with the greatest total, we have selected the Product that gives us the best possible chance of making money.

Of course, someone who is not risk adverse might look at the much higher potential profit of $800,000 of Product 1 and might decide to "go for it."

Pareto Analysis

Pareto analysis uses Bar Charts to depict given situations, usually representing the occurrence of some quantity such as frequency, time, quantity or cost. This is different than the Pareto Rule that many people know as the 80-20 rule. The 80-20 rule states that often 80% of the certain events come from 20% of the causes. An example is that 80% of a country's income comes from 20% of its people.

But back to our bar charts. As an example, suppose that we want to determine the leading cause(s) of failure when using our PC. We gather data that shows that several PC repair shops list the following.

- Repair Shop 1 – Hard drive crashes 142 times; operating system software corrupted 78 times; screen burns out 12 times; power supply fails 24 times; telecommunications doesn't work 134 times; dropped liquid onto keyboard 44 times; battery failure 10 times.

- Repair Shop 2 – Hard drive crashes 97 times; operating system software corrupted 56 times; screen burns out 15 times; power supply fails 18 times; telecommunications doesn't work 175 times; dropped liquid onto keyboard 12 times; battery failure 3 times.

- Repair Shop 3 – Hard drive crashes 122 times; operating system software corrupted 76 times; screen burns out 5 times; power supply fails 13 times; telecommunications doesn't work 112 times; dropped liquid onto keyboard 33 times; battery failure 15 times.

We can add the results from all three Repair Shops. This gives us the total number of failures for this sample set.

- <u>Total PC Failures</u> – Hard drive crashes 361 times; operating system software corrupted 210 times; screen burns out 32 times; power supply fails 55 times; telecommunications doesn't work 421 times; dropped liquid onto keyboard 89 times; battery failure 28 times.

Plotting this data in a bar chart with the biggest value on the left side and the smallest value on the right side yields Figure 8-8.

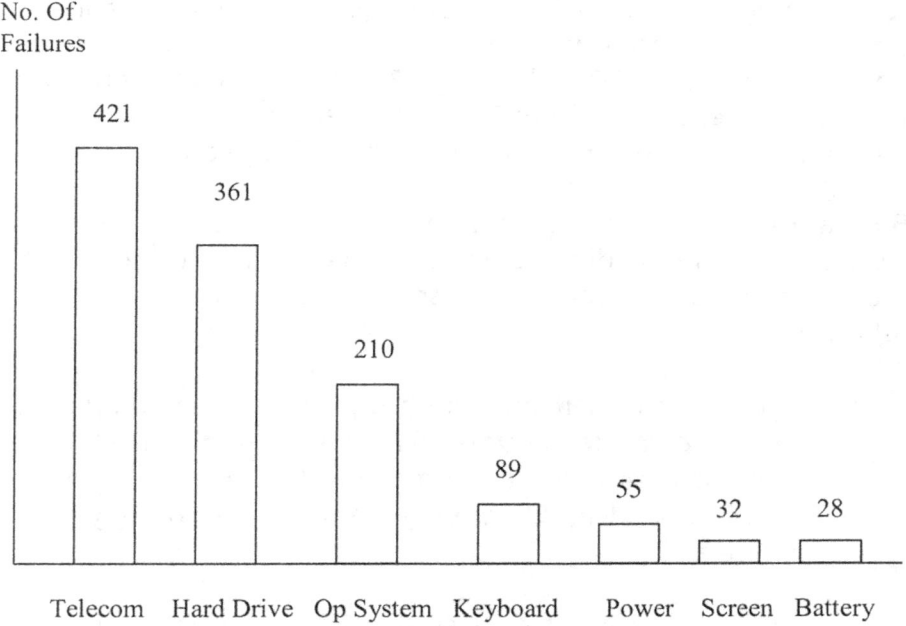

Figure 8-8 – Total Number of Each PC Component Failure

It is easy to see where the major effort needs to be placed to improve the failure rates of this set of PCs. Note that I have ignored replacement costs, etc., which should be taken into account to determine whether the problem solutions selected are cost- and time-effective.

Clustering

The concept of clustering data to make decisions can be a very powerful technique. By clustering, we mean we are looking for items that group together. There are many mathematical techniques that can be used to cluster data. We will not use any of them here. If you are interested, there are many books on the subject. Instead, we will look at data we gather (using the approaches in the following chapters) to see if the data groups (clusters) together.

Let's take a whimsical example of clustering. Suppose you bought a can of mixed nuts which contained cashews, peanuts and almonds. You want to run an experiment to determine if you can get a machine to distinguish among them just by measuring weight and volume of each nut. You measure these 2 properties for each nut in the can. In this Figure 8-9, the "t" = peanuts; the "x" = cashews, and the "o" = almonds.

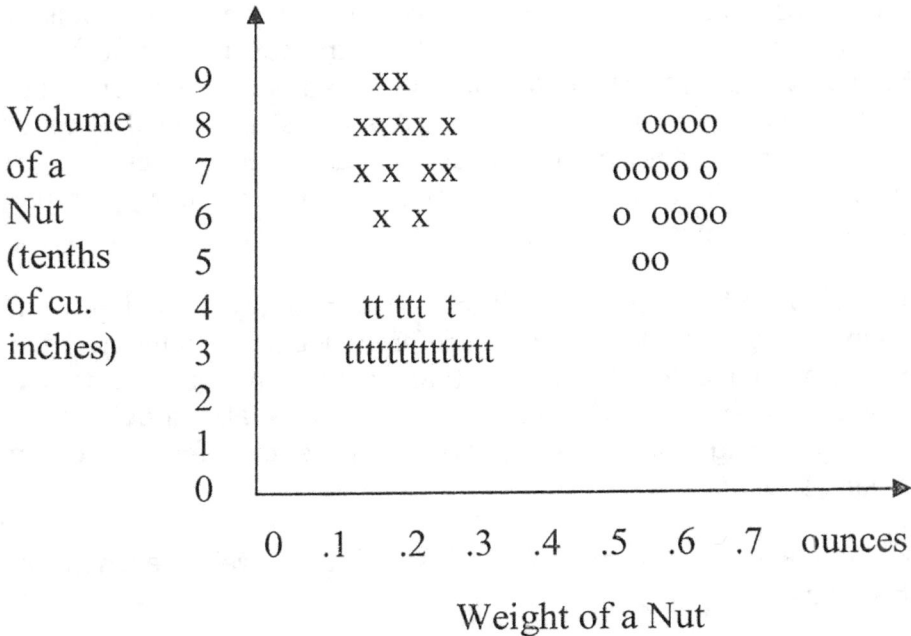

Figure 8-9 – Clustering Approach to Separate Different Types of Nuts

We see that the samples with the same marks group together, therefore we can automatically sort and count the nuts. This is our concept of clustering. This approach applies to many problems and is one element of a technical subject area called Pattern Recognition.

Pattern Recognition is used in many of Our Systems World activities daily and in general we are not aware that it is occurring. When we try to identify different people in a group we are looking for visual clues such as hair color, facial features, sound of their voice, etc. We are applying pattern recognition. If we are trying to determine the projected demographics of an area, we are looking at many different factors and then we are applying pattern recognition. Other examples include differentiating among different songs, cars, food, medical conditions, stock market trends and so on.

Which Tool Do I Use?

I have introduced eight possible decision tools that we can use in helping us make our decision. The choice of which tool or tools to use is a personal choice and depends on the specific problem, our familiarity with using the different tools, whether we have some tool set that allows less effort to arrive at the decision, as well as other factors. So some decision makers use one or two tools because they feel comfortable with the results or because the tool closely matches the way they think.

As you looked at the tools and their examples you probably got a feeling for which tool might match different decision situations. I have put together a table in Figure 8-10 that looks at some of the factors to consider when we decide which tool to use. This table should guide us in narrowing down the tool(s) we could use for different decision making situations.

In Figure 8-10 I have used the following criteria to weight each box in this figure.

- 4 = very applicable
- 2 = applicable
- 0 = not applicable

This figure, of course, is a simple decision matrix.

Decision Making Characteristics	Simple Pro/Con	Force Field Analysis	Simple Decision Table	Weighted Decision Table	Normal Decision Tree	Weighted Decision Tree	Pareto Analysis	Clustering
Analyzing frequency data	0	0	2	2	0	0	4	2
Factors have different levels of importance	0	4	0	4	0	4	2	2
Decision based on several criteria	4	4	4	4	2	4	2	4
Narrowing options to one choice	2	2	4	4	4	4	4	4
Yes/No decisions	4	4	2	2	0	0	2	2
Easy to generate	4	4	4	2	2	0	4	0
Prioritizes options	0	2	4	4	0	4	4	0
Identify possible paths to decision options	0	0	0	2	4	4	0	0
Need to group elements	2	2	4	4	2	2	2	4

Figure 8-10 – A Comparison of Decision Making Tools
for Different Problems

I use this table to help eliminate tools that are not applicable to the analysis under consideration.

Then I try to determine the complexity of the problem and eliminate those that are too complex to use (at least for the initial analysis – sometimes we have to go back and use the complicated approach if the initial attempts do not yield a decision). For example, if the data that I need to use would produce a decision tree with dozens and dozens of branches or more, I would eliminate this approach (unless I have automated tools to assist in keeping track of the branches).

Finally I prioritize the remaining tools and select the best, apply it to the problem, and make my decision. If this tool does not produce a clear cut choice, I add additional characteristics if they exist and redo the analysis. If this doesn't yield a clear cut decision, I select the next best tool and apply it.

In Part III, we look at the details on how to apply what we have learned in Parts I and II to plan, analyze, determine, and implement our problem solving and decision making skills in Our Systems World.

PART III
—
SYSTEMS THINKING
AND
PROBLEM SOLVING
IN
MY SYSTEMS WORLD

STEP BY STEP BY STEP BY STEP BY STEP: *THE 5 STEPS OF SYSTEMS THINKING AND PROBLEM SOLVING*

Stepping Out

U p to this point, we have introduced the concepts of My Systems World, systems and strategic thinking, and tools that we can use to solve problems, identify opportunities and make decisions. Now I will present a step by step procedure that we can use as the basis of attacking any problem that arises in Our Systems World. It is important to remember that as we go through each step, we are making decision after decision.

There are five steps that make up what I call **The Framework for Systems Thinking & Problem Solving in My Systems World**. As before, all of these techniques apply to individuals as well as organizations.

The five steps in the Framework are:

- Step 1: Defining the Problem and Thinking Strategically
- Step 2: Goal Setting and Planning
- Step 3: Analyzing the Situation
- Step 4: Determining and Implementing the Solution
- Step 5: Evaluating and Updating My Systems World

In the following chapters, we discuss each of these steps, what they mean, and how to use them. As we go through the steps we see that the amount of effort and the level of thinking will vary significantly depending on the problem. Many problems that we attack on a day-by-day basis may require only a fraction of the capabilities supplied by the individual steps. The amount of analysis required and the time needed to make our decisions may be very short. At the other extreme, problems encountered by organizations may require thousands of hours to work the problem and arrive at a solution. These situations may require significant resources of people, money, and facilities before the best solution is correctly implemented.

Another important point is that once you complete a step, that step does not disappear. It may be necessary to go back to earlier steps and update them as we learn more about our problems and our solutions. Remember our earlier discussion of feedback and feed forward. Those concepts apply in any problem we are solving and any decisions we are making (see Figure 9-1).

Some Key Points to get the Juices Flowing

Before we look at the five steps in detail, here are several key points that we will elaborate on in the following chapters. These points will guide us as we go through the information presented in those chapters.

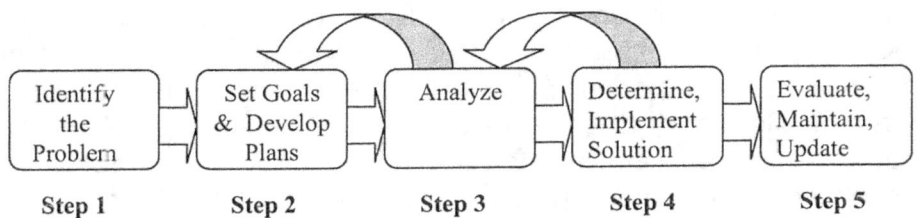

Figure 9-1 – Framework for Systems Thinking and Problem Solving

Point 1 (from Step 1) – Solve the right problem

We must first have a clear understanding of what we are trying to accomplish. Time after time as I have reviewed both small and enterprise-wide projects with costs ranging from tens of thousands to hundreds of millions of dollars, I have found that as the problems were worked and decisions made, there were many disasters because the wrong problem was being solved. The person or teams of people lost sight of what was to be accomplished, and spent enormous amounts of resources producing useless results.

As an example, suppose the problem is to improve the way an organization does business. This would entail identifying the functions that an organization must do to improve their operation and to determine the best ways to do that. Instead, the problem actually solved was the replacement of information technology components (e.g., computers) to make the information processing faster. The analyses and solutions may have looked great, but the results desired weren't achieved. Just replacing IT gear usually is not the solution to the problem.

We can read about many different projects that spent hundreds of millions of dollars, but were finally abandoned because the project did not satisfy the systems needs. This is one of the reasons why I took the time in Parts I and II discussing the systems thinking approach to problem solving. For any problem, we need to look at the big picture and the interactions that can occur in Our Systems World.

If the problem we are solving is complex or if our decision has many factors, do as we discussed in Part 1 and break the problem/system down into its components; and into sub-components if necessary. If the problem or decision consists of several different problems or decisions, we may want to determine if one or more of the problems or decisions are more important than the others. In other words, prioritize the problems or decisions if we can. We can the break it down into more coherent parts. If we can't prioritize, then we can apply our systems thinking approach to the total problem or decision.

So we have to correctly define what we are trying to accomplish while being aware of our environment, in other words, of Our Systems World. It may require us to expand Our Systems World to include the added requirements and elements (or entities) needed to identify and solve the problem.

Point 2 (from Step 1) – Understand our environment

Think back to Part I, Systems Thinking and My Systems World, and again consider our systems thinking concepts. We have to be alert to Our Systems World and the linkages that can be involved as a result of our decision. There is a basic question that we often consider when looking at a linked environment. That is, because of our decision, who, what, where, when, how many (persons or entities) will be affected? We need to determine if this decision will expand Our Systems World to include additional entities.

Point 3 (from Step 2) - Take the pertinent factors into account in making our decision, but not irrelevant factors

This is very important in determining the scope or magnitude of what we are going to analyze. We have to look for important information that can help us solve our problem or make our decision. Included are factors that might cause a problem if they were missed or ignored.

With the amazing amount of data available to us, it is useless and time consuming to look at and analyze data that can't help us. This data "overload" will bog us down and may lead to poor decisions.

A simple way of saying this is *focus on the real problem and ignore the rest*. Suppose, for example, that we are trying to determine how to restructure all the financial functions in our organization. We need to determine the organization's Systems World and identify only those elements that are pertinent to the financial functions. This is not easy since our clients, staffing, physical location resources, etc., can all be relevant – or not. This is a very important activity <u>before</u> data collection begins. On occasion, we might start to collect data and then realize that some of the directions in which we are headed are irrelevant. Stop that specific data collection and refine what we really need.

Again, I have seen many projects that have run out of time because the people running the project became involved in gathering "all the data" that they could associated with the problem area, before they started analyzing what they had gathered.

Point 4 (from Step 3) - Factor in any uncertainties and identify the pertinent risk factors

Let's look at the concept of Risk verses Reward. We need to determine if the reward that we will receive is worth the risk that is needed to achieve that reward. This is often called your risk tolerance. Risk is a part of every decision that we make. Often these risks are small and inconsequential. However, there are decisions that we make that are very significant to our well being or the well being of others, perhaps even to the point of reaching the life/death decision.

If risks are to be important to us, we then have to be able to determine what the risks are and ways to control or manage them. Today there are techniques and tools available to do this as I discuss in Step 3.

Point 5 (from Step 3) - Determine if there are alternative solutions and decisions that we can make.

Think about the possible outcomes of our decision. Perform a simple "What-If" analysis. What-If analysis is where we try to determine <u>what</u> might happen <u>if</u> we take certain actions. Will we then achieve our goals? What-If we did something else? Would the results be better or worse? Are some results more acceptable than others in our environment? Does this make a difference in our decisions?

For example, what if I invested resources to purchase a competitor? Can I assimilate that organization into my operations? Which of their products or services will I retain, sell or discard? And so on.

Suppose, instead, I invested those resources to develop our own products and services. Would this outcome help me reach my goals easier and faster?   For any problem area, there are many more questions that we need to answer, but this approach is still applicable to both simple and complex analyses.

Point 6 (from Step 3) - Can the results we want be achieved?

Is what we want to do feasible? What are the obstacles? Feasibility analysis can help us determine what can be achieved or help to reshape the problem. In Step 3, I present a list of feasibility concerns and look at how we can check for the different feasibilities.

Point 7 (from Step 4) – What actions should we take?

Hopefully by this stage in our analysis, we have chosen the approach to solving the problem and arriving at a decision. Now we need to determine additional factors such as:

- What resources are required?
- Are their any time restrictions?
- What detailed actions need to be taken?

These are discussed in more detail in Step 4.

Point 8 (from Step 5) – Evaluating our decisions.

Monitor the outcomes of our decisions. Were the problems resolved successfully? Were there interactions that we didn't consider? Should we reevaluate and make changes?

When we make a decision, based on what we know, we may have made a very good decision, but the outcomes of our decision may not be what we hoped for. That doesn't make it a bad decision. Sometimes there are factors under which we have no control. Just assess what the state of the situation is and try to make what happens next more to our liking.

Similarly, if we make bad decisions and the outcomes of our decisions are good, take what we get and move on. Never-the-less, the chances that we get what we want are better when we make good decisions.

Getting Ready for the 5 Steps

Look at the big picture (our systems thinking approach) and the interactions with the outside world. Then continue and break the problem into smaller pieces just as we did with Our Systems World environment. Then analyze each piece as well as the interactions among the pieces that are of importance in making a decision. Then combine our different analysis conclusions and come up with a decision.

We should keep the important and pertinent information that we learned and gathered during our analyses for future decisions and problem solving.

CHAPTER 10

STEP 1 –THINK THINK THINK: *DEFINING THE PROBLEM AND THINKING STRATEGICALLY*

Go For the Gold – Solve the Right Problem

In the previous Chapter, our first key point was entitled **Solve the right problem**. This is an idea that seems so obvious that many would think that it is not even worth mentioning, let alone identifying it as a key point in the Systems Thinking Approach to solving problems in My Systems World. WRONG! If we do not properly define what we are attempting to do, we WILL NOT get the results that we hoped for, no matter how much time and effort that we put into coming up with the "right" answer. So Think Think Think about the problem at hand.

How do we know that we have a problem to begin with? There are many ways that this can come about. We may be unhappy with the way things are and want to find a better way to do things. It may be identifying a better personal opportunity in Our Systems World such as our employment, social relationships, education, health or whatever. It may be a problem with our company's product or products as identified by our customers. Our company's profit outlook may be dimming in the face of new technology or labor problems. Suppose there is a crisis in our organization? Perhaps there was an environmentally sensitive accident that requires both rapid response and media attention. In these case, clearly a problem exists.

So we need to determine what it is that we want to accomplish. Once we can identify what our problem is, we need to clearly express it in written form. As we look at Our Systems World, we must try to determine what might change in Our Systems World and whether Our Systems World will modify what we are trying to accomplish. There is nothing wrong with modifying our problem definition as we work through this thinking process and learn more.

A Man (or Woman) On a Mission – Problem Solving in Our Systems World

No matter whether we are individuals or are members of a corporation, there is a structured way to look at trying to determine what to do in Our Systems World. Specifying, in high-level terms, what we want to accomplish, where we are starting from, our value system, and perhaps how to get there can be considered our mission. A simple way to look at the meaning of the word mission is that a mission is nothing more than an overall goal. We must identify what we want to do or the problem that we want to solve. For an organization, the mission is further defined as a statement of the organization's unique purpose that tends to distinguish the organization from other organizations in its same work area.

An example of a mission might be the following. "Our mission is to build a personal services firm that will provide high quality technical analyses in the telecommunications field to support the federal government." To be able to satisfy our mission, we will need long-term and short-term goals and the associated plans. Our long-term goals are called strategic goals and the plans that are derived are called strategic plans. Similarly, our short-term goals are called tactical goals and produce tactical plans. Finally there is a need to put into place the action plan identifying what actions we are going to take. This plan is often called an operational plan. These concepts are illustrated in Figure 10-1.

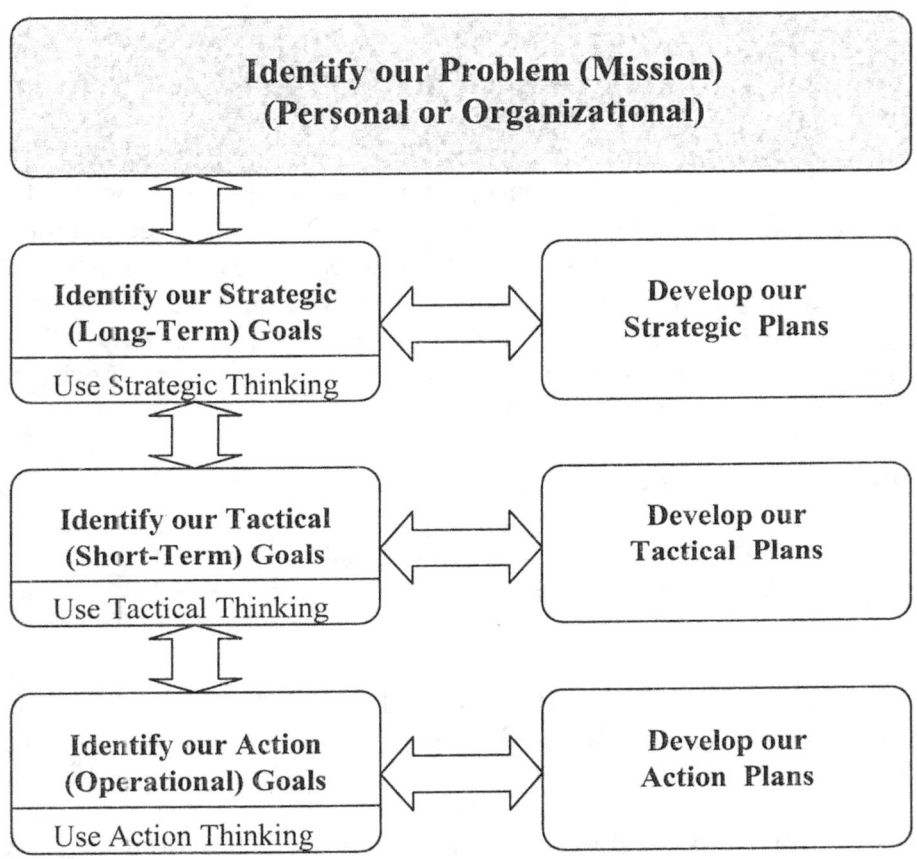

Figure 10-1 – Systems Thinking in Our Systems World

I like to think of each problem, the procedures to solving that problem, and the problem solution as a "Project". Therefore for each problem or mission we identify, we have the corresponding project. A simple project can have just a few activities that we need to solve our problem, or it can be very complex, requiring the use of significant and detailed planning, analysis and implementation.

If I Do This, What Will Happen? – Scenario Analysis

If we take some action, what will the final outcome be? For many of our problems in Our Systems World, we don't know for sure. There may be several possible outcomes for every action we take, some more likely than others. Scenario Analysis attempts to look to the future to determine what might happen when we take specific actions. It is applying our systems thinking concepts to possible future outcomes.

A good scenario analysis is based on many factors. First one has to have a feel for the problem and possible solutions. This feeling may occur based on the individual's or team's experiences, or on pertinent data gathered and analyzed to determine possible outcomes. Decision making tools given in Part II can help in this analysis. We can use the data gathered and analysis performed using our decision tools to help generate our scenarios.

What we would like are answers to questions such as:

- If we do this, then the outcome is that.
- If we do that, then the outcome is something else that we can specify

The greater the confidence that we will get the desired outcome for a given input, the higher the probability that the desired outcome will occur.

As we attempt to get closer to identifying the final outcome, we may have to prioritize several potential outcomes. To improve the chance of getting to the right outcome, we try to more precisely define our problem, goals and plans.

Sometimes other factors come into play after we have defined our problem. A listing of our possible outcomes relative to the quality of our problem definition is as follows:

- Case 1 – Good problem definition yields good outcome
- Case 2 – Good problem definition yields bad outcome
- Case 3 – Bad problem definition yields good outcome
- Case 4 – Bad problem definition yields bad outcome

Cases 1 and 4 appear reasonable in that a good problem definition should yield a good outcome and a bad problem definition should yield a bad outcome. Cases 2 and 3 are not as clear. As an example of

Case 2, an investor decided to build and open a family entertainment center near my neighborhood. It seemed like a good investment in that the investor had built an entertainment center before and had the experience to make it successful. There are no other centers of that size and variety anywhere within a large geographic area. After beginning construction, a hurricane hit our area and created significant damage. This resulted in the center's construction workers quitting and going to other jobs at a higher pay, thereby bringing construction on the center to a halt. As the workers started to become free a year later, another hurricane occurred resulting in further delay as well as significant increases in materials costs. The final construction date was therefore push backed over 3 years from the planned date resulting in bankruptcy for the investor. Here a good problem definition certainly resulted in a bad outcome for all involved, including the community.

You can probably come up with your own example of Case 3. These usually occur when something good unexpectedly happens.

We discuss project goals and plans in this and the following chapters. We begin below talking about the Strategic Goals and Strategic Plans.

Strategy to the Rescue

As discussed earlier in the book, we looked at systems thinking in Our Systems World. We saw that our strategic thinking included taking a broad overview of our thinking and our interactions within Our Systems World. I call this broad-based initial thinking strategic thinking. In My Systems World, strategic thinking is part of systems thinking. We therefore see that strategic thinking tries to look into the future and determine what we need to do and how we need to do it on a high-level. Systems thinking, on the other hand, encompasses strategic thinking and a lot more. It looks not only at the overall Systems World and the associated links among the systems involved with solving the problem at hand, but it also includes mission statements, identification of goals, individual task planning (and how the task interacts with other tasks), detailed task and systems analysis, potential actions to be taken, and evaluation of the results of actions taken.

Let's take a trip back in time to see an example of strategic thinking. We are going to the mid to late 19th century. This was a time of turmoil in the world. In Europe, battles were being fought among many of the European states. From the military we get the word **strategy** meaning generalship. A famous military strategist was a general named Helmuth Karl von Moltke, referred to as Moltke the Elder since he had a famous son with the same name. Moltke the Elder was a chief of the Prussian and German general staffs.

Moltke engineered, over many years, the strategies behind the military victories that led to the assembly of independent German states into the German Empire in 1871. The way that he did this was by thinking about the different possible battles that might take place in the future and identifying ways to win these battles. When a similar situation arose he was ready to act quickly and decisively. This approach to looking at what possible situations might present themselves in the future is what we called scenario analysis.

So Moltke the Elder possessed several characteristics that he employed to generate his strategic positions. He could understand the significance of certain events, think about possible actions and outcomes, make decisions quickly and take the decided action without hesitation to achieve his predetermined goals. These characteristics are important elements when employing strategic thinking, and they are often used today by successful persons to determine where they should be headed and how to get there.

There are many nuances when discussing strategy in Our Systems World. Therefore let us take strategy (as shown in Figure 10-2) to mean:

- a good understanding of where you want to go in the future, and
- a clear description of the important elements in Your Systems World that will impact your outcome(s), and
- a pathway to get from here to there - while understanding the potential problems and how to avoid them.

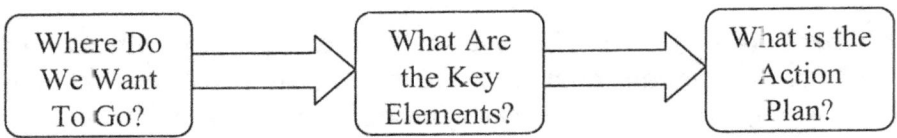

Figure 10-2 – Strategic Thinking

Hence, in the military we can think of strategy as the planning and directing of large military forces to achieve the stated goals and objectives. By extending strategic concepts to Our Systems World, we think of strategy as the path to achieve what we want. In Our Business Systems World, the strategy tells us where the enterprise wants to be by a certain time, which services or products the enterprise will bring to the marketplace, and how the enterprise will accomplish this.

The need for a strategy becomes apparent as we think about the connections and linkages in Our Systems World. As we make decisions, many elements in Our Systems World are affected, both in the near-term and in the future. If we do not have a strategy, then our decisions and actions today might adversely affect our future interests.

To be able to see how the strategy can work, we can generate a strategic plan. An individual's strategic plan can be quite complex, especially if an individual continues to modify and refine the strategic plan throughout the person's lifetime. Few individuals do this and often find themselves going in directions that lead to dead ends – in their jobs, in their relationships, in their financial well being. Their life can become time wasting, money wasting, relationships wasting.

Corporations and other enterprises often generate strategic plans. A very important point is that this plan needs to be an active plan where changes are made on a regular basis. A plan that is generated and put on the shelf is both useless and harmful because it does not guide the enterprise in the direction that the key players in the organization want it to go. In fact, it can hinder progress because it can be referred back to by officers and personnel in the enterprise, and decisions are made on old and irrelevant directions.

So what is the difference between a strategic plan and other types of plans? A strategic plan looks to the future while considering the present, but on a significantly larger scale than a typical plan to achieve a short-term task. A strategic plan therefore contains directions for many, many tasks, as opposed to a tactical plan that normally addresses what and how to successfully achieve a single task.

The ideas presented in the following chapters (Steps 2, 3, 4 and 5) apply to strategic as well as tactical and action plans. All types of plans outline what has to be done by when and how. A plan will give direction to both an individual and anyone else involved in the individual's Systems World. In an organization, it will give direction to the management and staff. It is further critical that all parties involved understand and buy into the plan, be it strategic, tactical or action. This can be accomplished by involving the people that have a stake in the outcomes, i.e., people or organizations in Our Systems World. This includes our customers, management, family members, and other organizations if they are or will become part of Our Systems World.

Another interesting benefit of a strategic plan is that it can help us prioritize our activities. We all are driven by things that have to be done now – "the fire-drills" we all have on a daily basis. If we look at our strategic plan on a regular basis (e.g., once a week), it can often tell us what is *really* important so we know where to allocate our resources. Again, this is applicable to individuals as well as enterprises.

We will describe strategic plans in more detail in the next chapter after we discuss setting goals in Our Systems World.

CHAPTER 11

STEP 2 - A GOOD PLAN IS MORE THAN A PLAN: *GOAL SETTING & PLANNING*

Only One Plan Does Not a Good Pudding Make

In Step 1 in the previous chapter, we identified the concepts of strategic thinking, strategic goals, and strategic plans. We now expand on those concepts and discuss the additional goals and plans needed to permit the problem to be solved or the mission to be accomplished.

We need to learn to identify new situations and problems, and determine how we can attack and solve those problems in the best way. The best way often entails determining how the new situation fits into our personal or professional goals in Our Systems World, or into the goals of the enterprise. It is important as we develop our goals and plans to take into account **only** those factors that are pertinent to making a decision and solving a problem.

In Our Systems World, we know that any action that we take can affect many persons, places and things since these are linked together. It is important to look both at the near-term actions that we can take as well as at the long-term consequences of our actions. In reality we are planning for the future, but are also concerned with the near term steps and action that need to be taken.

In this chapter we will look at ways to identify goals and see how to develop plans to achieve the goals.

Where Do We Want to Go? Let's Get to the Goal Line

Using our strategic thinking ideas that we developed in the previous chapter, we can now determine what goals we need to achieve to implement our strategic plan. In the past, we all have had goals that we wanted to accomplish. Sometimes we wrote them down; sometimes we didn't. Simplistically, our New Year's Resolutions can be thought of as goals that we want to reach, e.g., losing weight, doing more exercises, getting promoted, starting a business, or moving our enterprise into a new market. Usually these are near-term goals, made without considering the consequences that could occur in Our Systems World.

So goals can help us in several different ways.

- Goals can provide directions to us, as individuals or as members of a team, which we can use to understand what is needed and where we are headed.

- A goal can become a rallying cry for a team of people. It helps generate team spirit and can get everyone involved heading in the same direction.

- Goals can help us develop quality plans for achieving the goals. If we use our systems thinking concept again, achieving our first set of goals may become the foundation for future goals.

- Goals can help us evaluate where we are, how we are doing in solving the problem, identifying changes we may need to make, and determining whether we are using our resources efficiently and effectively.

I am suggesting that we need to think about where we want to be both in the near-term and the long-term and to write these goals down. We can add, drop and modify these goals anytime we want. We also need to continue to remind ourselves of these goals (assuming that we are serious in achieving our goals) by reviewing these goals at least once a week so as to not lose sight of where we want to be.

The goals therefore will help us develop the Strategic Plan. Some examples of goals are the following.

- Goal # 1 – To increase the sales of our product by 12 % within the next 9 months

- Goal # 2 – To be accepted by Harvard or Yale Law School by March 15 of next year.

Since a goal is something that we want to achieve, we need to identify how, where and when we are going to achieve our goals. Unless we specify these details, the chance is slight that we will achieve what we set out to do. Specifying a detailed path to get from here to there will significantly increase our chances of success.

To make achieving our goal easier, our goal can be divided into smaller parts called sub-goals. When all of the sub-goals are completed, the goal is reached. Sub-goals are sometimes formulated because achieving a goal can be very difficult and complex and can appear overwhelming. By breaking the goal into smaller, more easily achievable sub-goals, a person can feel that they are moving forward as they achieve their sub-goals. This is another example of the systems thinking concept where large things are divided into more manageable smaller things. So dividing a goal will yield multiple sub-goals. For each sub-goal we generate a sub-goal plan. Each sub-goal plan produces an action goal and action plan. Each action plan now guides the actions taken to satisfy the sub-goal (see Figure 11-1). At each step of the way, feedback can occur to reinforce or modify the goals, sub-goals, plans and actions.

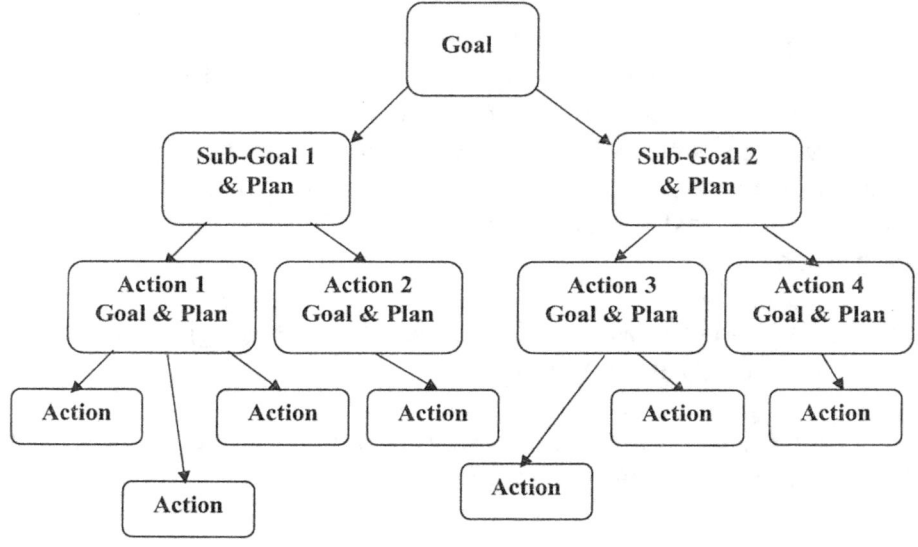

Figure 11-1 – Reaching Our Goal

It is important not to let failure stop us. Some people worry that they can't get it right. Just keep working toward our goals and we will get better at achieving our goals. Experience helps. We need to develop a TO-DO list for each goal that includes the following.

- Decide on our goals; if they involve others, get agreement

- Put each of our goals on a separate sheet of paper (or on our computer, etc.)
  o   A goal can have several sub-goals

- Prioritize our goals and sub-goals

- Limit the number of goals and the number of sub-goals so we won't get overwhelmed

- Develop decision criteria to determine how to recognize when we have achieved our goals

- Look over our goals on a regular basis to see how we are progressing

The Future Is Now – A Good Plan in Time Saves Nine

As we think about generating our different plans, we often do not give them the importance that they deserve. That may be because we really don't know what the future holds, therefore, why spend significant effort in generating plans. The answer to that feeling is clear. A bad plan can waste our time and resources and can sabotage achieving our goals. Hence "The Future Is Now" tells us that what we do now can affect our future in possibly many significant and critical ways. So let's put good plans together at all levels as we get to the appropriate points in the problem's life cycle.

Now we have to figure out how to achieve those goals. We need to generate long-term, near-term, and action plans.

Our long-term planning (our strategic plan) helps us think about where we want to be in 6 months or more and to identify possible ways to get there. We all need this long-term (strategic) plan. Again, we can change this long-term plan as things change in our life and in Our Systems World. Our short-term planning (called task planning or tactical planning) helps us determine what we need to do today, tomorrow, next week and during the next several months. Our action plan tells us how to do what we want to do. To be successful in Our Systems World, we need to develop all three sets of goals and generate all three plans.

A sample plan outline for each of the 3 plans is presented in the Appendix to this chapter.

Let us elaborate on our action plans and the actual actions taken. No matter how good a plan we have, we have to execute the plan properly.

Successful execution requires us to effectively follow our plan, properly use our resources, make good decisions when needed, and determine if we are accomplishing what we are trying to do. Good task management is therefore needed with schedules, personnel and other resources being effectively controlled. I will discuss task management in Step 4.

We often hear the expression "Operational Plans" when discussing planning within an organization. The expression Operational Plans can mean one of two different types of plans. The first plan type is nothing more than a different name for our action plans. This is often referred to as a "single-use" plan.

The second type of Operational Plans is called "standing-plans". These plans are put into place and remain there until changed. Included in this type of plan are items such as:

- Policies – an organization's general response to specific situations

- Standard operating procedures – ways that we will do things step-by-step in particular situations

There should not be any confusion when looking at a particular "Operational Plan" as to which definition is being used.

So let's think of our planning as helping us achieve our goals, i.e., to move from where we are now to where we want to be in the future. But since we see that the various elements in Our System World are interconnected, we must also take into account social, financial, health, business and time impacts of getting from here to there. A good plan should let us use the resources available to us in the most effective way.

It is important to note that the best plan for us might not be the best plan for someone else. Business planning for a company may be vastly different than an individual's personal plan, but the need for planning is the same. As a point of discussion, a business strategic plan often identifies the need for the organization to build a competitive advantage and to put in place the mechanisms to be able to maintain, extend and exploit that advantage. This business strategy might be applicable to an individual in the work environment, or even extended into personal relations.

Goals and Plans Together – A Nice Couple

As we develop our plans to meet our goals, we often get good ideas while we are doing something else: watching TV, taking a shower, and eating lunch. We want to add those ideas to our plans, so I recommend that we take our computer (or several pieces of paper) and generate the plan given in Figure 11-2. We might never fill in all the details in this plan, but we should capture all our thoughts and analysis and fill in whatever information we have that is applicable to our plan. In Step 3, several of the areas will be covered in more detail such as Requirements and Feasibility.

OUR PLAN FOR GOAL NUMBER ___

- Project Goal
- Strategic (Long-term) Goal & Plan
- Tactical (Short-term) Goal & Plan
- Action (Operational) Goal & Plan
- Requirements
- Feasibility
- Risks
- Alternatives
- Schedule and Resources
- Important data and data sources

Figure 11-2 – A Project Plan for a Given Goal

So we should continue to fill in additional areas as we proceed in our problem solving steps. We should continue to develop these plans as we learn more. Our plan should be dynamic! NEVER make a plan and put it on the shelf! Many organizations do just that, but good planning maintained in a current state can greatly enhance the performance of an individual or enterprise.

Oops! Something Went Wrong

No matter how much we plan, there is a good chance that something will go wrong. In each of our plans (strategic, tactical, action), we should build in "work arounds" for critical parts in our plans. These work arounds are what we call contingency planning. These alternate courses of actions should be determined before the plan is put into place. However, as we progress through a plan, we often determine potential problems that we weren't aware of when we started. So we can add to our contingency plan at any time in the project life cycle. We need to identify, for these critical parts, what to do, how to do it, resources and time required, and other effects to Our Systems World.

One area where this type of problem occurs is when we are trying to estimate the capabilities of new technologies that we plan to use. Sometimes these aren't ready or don't perform as expected. Have a contingency plan to handle this.

In some cases, good things happen. On one project that I was involved with, I identified a new technology in a research lab that hadn't been reported to the public. This new technology allowed several steps in our plans to be leapfrogged resulting in a much better system in a much shorter time.

But We Never Did It That Way

In attempting to develop and implement goals and plans, we usually run into barriers or roadblocks. At one extreme, we must develop goals and plans that can be accomplished using the time and resources available. We need to determine if any constraints exist that would prove insurmountable or costly. We must also determine if we are naive and do not understand the complexity of what we are trying to accomplish. Finally, we should determine if what we are doing is appropriate for our organization, i.e., are we doing something that would appear to conflict with good and ethical practices.

At the other extreme, we may run into staff resistance. The resistance can take on many forms and can result from:

- Poor communication of the mission, goals and plans

- Typical resistance to change – we have never done it that way (or we have always done it a different way)

- Individuals' concerns over their future roles and/or compensation

- Resisting any activity where an individual's performance can be measured against some sort of schedule or goal

Some or all of these concerns should be addressed before the action plan is put into effect. It is easier and less costly to change things before we start, or early in the process, rather than later in the project's life cycle. Again, a project life cycle is nothing more than all the activities that occur within a project from the project's start until it is completed.

STRATEGIC PLANS, TACTICAL PLANS AND ACTION PLANS OUTLINES WE CAN USE

Background Information

This Appendix provides an outline for each of the three plans which we discussed in this Chapter 11, i.e., Strategic Plans, Tactical Plans and Action Plans. It is important to note that each plan (e.g., Strategic Plan), can have many different formats depending on the person or the organization developing the plan. The complexity of the plans will also differ because of what each organization wants to accomplish. A plan can provide very detailed information in each of the sections or it can provide just minimal information based on the person's or organization's needs.

As we work toward achieving a given goal, we develop additional details of what we want to accomplish and how to do it. These additional details are presented in our plans and divided into Objectives and Actions (sometimes called strategies). The more details that we can generate on what we are going to do and how we are going to do it, the better chance we have of achieving our goal.

As an example of developing our goals and objectives, I include a sample goal and some of the objectives we might use for developing increased business in our organization. (Refer to Figure 11-1.)

Goal 1: Become the number one supplier of secure telecommunication services in the US.

Sub-Goal 1.1 - Increase secure telecommunication services provided to Federal and state governments

- Objective 1.1.1 – Continue to expand Federal government business
    - increase government business totaling $__ M by adding __ new agencies within 6 months
    - win Telecommunication Master Contract currently out for bid

- Objective 1.1.2 – Initiate business development activities with state governments
    - Participate in __ major trade shows/conferences this year frequented by key government employees
    - Meet with __ new clients per month

Sub-Goal 1.2 - Increase secure telecommunication services provided to Mid-Size Corporations

Sub-Goal 1.3 - Acquire selected telecommunications security firms

Each of these items can be expanded further to get to more detailed levels. A format like this can be used in each of our plans.

Plan Outlines

The outlines which I present below can be modified to meet the needs of the user and should be used as a guideline. Many Strategic Plans only need to complete *Part 2: General Plan* to produce a useful plan.

Strategic Planning

This Strategic Plan Outline is oriented toward a corporate environment, but can be adapted to an individual's needs.

A Sample Strategic Plan Outline

Part 1: Overview

- Summary
- Organization's Background
- Business Overview
  o   Organizational Structure and Business Systems
  o   Business Model
- Facilities
- Other Resources Available
- Products or Services Provided
  o   Current Status
- Marketplace Analysis
- Core Competencies
- Internal and External Networks
  o   People
  o   Systems

Part 2: General Plan

- Vision Statement
- Mission Statement
- Strategic Goals, Objectives and Strategies
- Problems and Opportunities
- Feasibilities, Costs and Benefits
- Assumptions
- Other Pertinent Information

Part 3: Specific Organizational Entities

- Marketing
  - o Strategic Goals, Objectives, Strategies
  - o Other Pertinent Information
    - Applicable networks
      - People
      - Systems
- Manufacturing
  - o Strategic Goals, Objectives, Strategies
  - o Other Pertinent Information
    - Applicable networks
      - People
      - Systems
- Finance
  - o Strategic Goals, Objectives, Strategies
  - o Other Pertinent Information
    - Applicable networks
      - People
      - Systems
- Research and Development
  - o Strategic Goals, Objectives, Strategies
  - o Other Pertinent Information
    - Applicable networks
      - People
      - Systems
- Information Technology
  - o Strategic Goals, Objectives, Strategies
  - o Other Pertinent Information
    - Applicable networks
      - People
      - Systems
- Other Elements (as Necessary)
  - o Strategic Goals, Objectives, Strategies
  - o Other Pertinent Information
    - Applicable networks
      - People
      - Systems

Part 4: Pertinent Supporting Information

Any information deemed important for this plan.

Tactical Planning

Our tactical plans are used to determine what needs to be done and how to do it in the near term, normally extending out about six months to a year, for a specified time, or until a specific action is completed. Our tactical plans usually deal with the personnel in charge of guiding other personnel to complete these plans. In an organization, these people often are identified as the mid-level managers. Hence, our tactical plans are the plans that attempt to satisfy the Tactical Goals derived from the Strategic Plan.

Our Tactical Plan can take on part of the form that we used in our Strategic Plan.

Tactical Plan Outline

- Tactical Goals, Objectives and Strategies
- Near-Term Problems and Opportunities
- Feasibilities, Costs and Benefits
- Assumptions
- Other Pertinent Information

Again, specific operational entities such as marketing, finance and human resources can each have their own tactical plan if the generation of such plans is needed.

For example, if we are looking at a Marketing Operation, several areas can be addressed. A sampling of some of these is as follows.

- Product descriptions
- Current and potential product uses
- Price structures and strategies
- Strengths and weaknesses of products
- Customer attitudes toward products
- How to increase client purchases

- Potential product improvements
- Sales history for different factors (e.g., geographical)
- Sales force available
- Distribution network
- Advertising and product placement
- Market direction
- Market share
- Competition and their strengths and weaknesses
- Financial trends

Action Plan (Operational Plan)

The specific actions expected from an individual or group is identified in the Action Plan and is derived from the Action Goals and the Tactical Plan. These actions are very specific, e.g., "Sign four new clients each week." This is an example of an on-going plan in that the specified action continues until it is changed. If our example was modified to say "Sign four new clients each week for three weeks," this is called a finite or single-use plan since once the time has passed, the action is no longer in effect.

Our Action Plan identifies specific actions and uses only a part of the outline that we used in our Strategic Plan.

Action Plan Outline

- Action Goals, Objectives and Strategies
- Near-Term Problems and Solutions
- Feasibilities, Costs and Benefits
- Assumptions
- Other Pertinent Information

Again, specific operational entities such as marketing, finance and human resources can each have their own action plan if the generation of such plans is needed. Some specific actions might include:

- Acquire resources needed
- Rapidly develop infrastructure if needed
- Specify interfaces

- Contact critical persons
- Conduct meetings, gather and analyze data
- Design system elements
- Manage personnel
- Acquire services and/or technologies
- Develop performance standards
- Track progress
- Evaluate results
- Secure data
- Model situations
- Perform analyses

These actions should lead to the desired outcome (solution) of the problem being addressed. I will discuss how to analyze the results of our actions and to obtain a solution in the next 2 chapters, i.e., in Steps 3 and 4.

Strategic Thinking Checklist

I am including another helpful concept to assist in generating our outcomes if we need to gather more data to help us focus on the problem. This example is used to better understand our client or customer at a strategic level, although it is useful at all plan levels. It essentially generates a checklist that can be used directly with the client.

The Client's Environment

1. Know and understand the Client's mission

   - Help the client understand the mission.
   - What is the history behind the mission?
   - What is the relevant legislation and public policy?
   - What is the entire context of the mission?

2. Define the specific problem

   - Is it an operational problem?
   - Technical problem?

- Political problem?
- Does the ultimate user perceive a problem?

3. Define the Goals and Objectives

4. Identify the Stakeholders and Motivations

- Congress
- Agency
- Public
- Users
- Contractors
- Employees

5. Identify the Driving Factors

- Reduce costs
- Improve service
- Introduce new services
- Implement new legislation

6. Identify the Resources Available

- How much money is involved?
- What is the source of the money?
- Are the right skills available?

These and other questions are generated before meeting with the client. In addition, we should try to answer these questions and address possible concerns ourselves before meeting with the client to better understand the client's responses.

CHAPTER 12

STEP 3 —WHAT DO WE NEED TO DO? *ANALYZING THE SITUATION*

Requirements, Feasibilities, Risks, Uncertainties, Alternatives, Consequences – WOW! No Wonder I'm Confused

In previous steps, we identified our strategic, tactical and action goals and plans. Using these goals and plans, we now detail what we need to do and how to do it. In other words, we analyze pertinent factors in Our Systems World to determine if they allow us to get where we want to go. We further look at the potential results of our actions to see if we get one or more (what we think are) good solutions to the problem we are working in Our Systems World. These possible solutions are the alternatives that we now investigate in more detail to determine if they really are good and viable solutions.

Let's Do It This Way

In determining our best alternative solutions to a problem and to get the details on how to implement our action plan, there are several steps that we go through. These steps are as follows:

- Step 3-1 – Determine what is needed by those in Our Systems World that are affected by the actions that we take. These are called the requirements for the solution.

- Step 3-2 – Analyze what is feasible in terms of meeting the requirements.

- Step 3-3 – Consider uncertainties that may occur during this process, the risks involved and our risk tolerance

- Step 3-4 – Use the decision making tools of Part II to help select possible alternative solutions to our problem

- Step 3-5 – Analyze the consequences resulting from our choice of a particular solution

- Step 3-6 – Select our alternatives

As we go through each of these steps and get information and answers, we should plug this information back into our Goal Plan that we discussed in the chapter 11 (Figure 11-2).

Step 3-1: Who Wants What? – Determining Requirements

Let's determine the requirements (needs) that we would have to satisfy to reach our goal. I like to break our requirements into five different parts as follows:

- User requirements
- Activity (functional) requirements
- Performance requirements
- Technical requirements
- Resource requirements

During our requirements determination we may need to gather information from other people or other sources (e.g., library, Internet, corporate manuals). I will discuss data and information gathering later.

User requirements determine what the users of the system need. In an enterprise, for example, what does the financial department personnel need to efficiently maintain and update the company financial records? For an individual attending a commuter college, what does the user need regarding transportation, financial support, time and baby sitters? There are usually many users involved when we are solving a problem in Our Systems World, and it is important to try to identify them and determine their needs. The visualization techniques that we presented earlier are useful in generating the user needs and their interactions with other needs.

Activity (functional) requirements are usually very important in successfully achieving a goal. The concept of an activity or function is not difficult, but few people think about using activity (functional) concepts.

Here's an example. Suppose you want to build a house. We may say something like this to our architect: "I want a house with three bedrooms, a living room, a dining room, a nice kitchen, two baths, perhaps a study, and a two-car garage."

But another way of looking at designing a house is to say that we need to satisfy the following functions: sleeping areas for four people, eating area, lounging area for ten people, bathing and toilet areas, cooking area, and an area to protect my two cars. Each of the verbs (e.g., sleeping, eating, cooking) are functions to be performed in the house, hence, a function is an activity. It is interesting that many well known architects design their buildings using functional requirements. Thinking this way can result in a more efficient house than the usual room specific approach. An example of this is shown in Figure 12-1.

Do we want the eating area and toilet area combined? I don't think so. Should Sleeping Area 3 be separated from the other major functions - perhaps as a separate casita? It is much easier to design the house layout using this approach. The more complicated the building, the more useful functional analysis becomes.

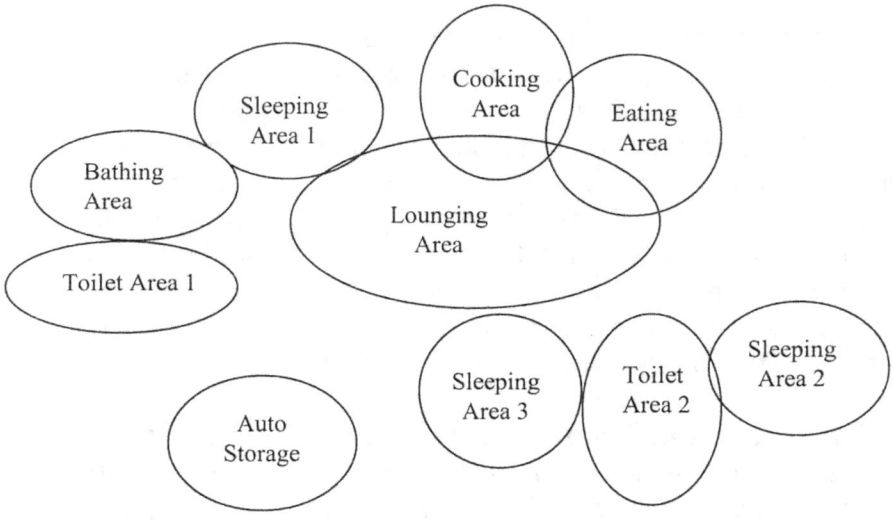

Figure 12-1– Our House Functions

Let me now give you an example of a simple business functional (activity) requirement. In this example, we have a company's customer paying their latest bill (see Figure 12-2).

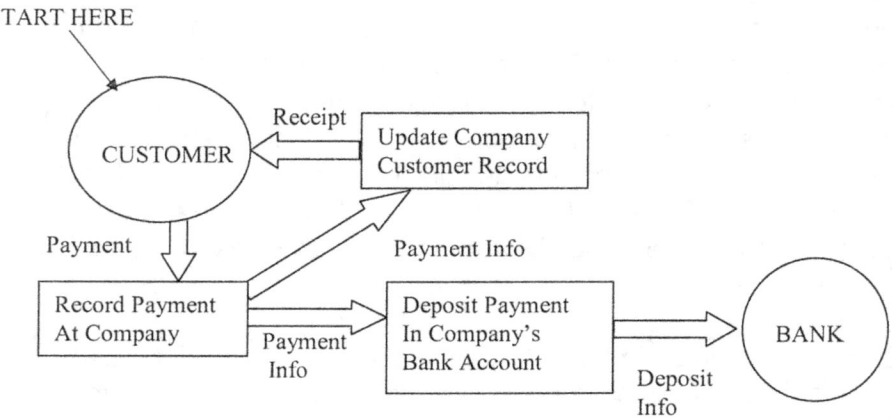

Figure 12-2 – A Business Activity (Functional) Requirement

I normally use CAPITAL LETTERS and ovals for things and lower case letters and rectangles for activities, so for this example CUSTOMER and BANK are things. These things are often called the sources or sinks (receivers) of data and information. It is helpful to use this notation, especially if our drawings become complex.

Just a quick point for businesses: these functional requirements can be used in corporate Business Process Reengineering and other development techniques to help in redesigning how a company does business.

Performance requirements are those that specify performance goals. Perhaps, someone needs a stove that can bake a standard size pie in one minute. Maybe someone else needs a computer that can perform a specified mathematical operation (e.g., invert a 10,000 by 10,000 matrix) in 0.003 seconds. These are performance requirements.

Technical requirements specify the technical capabilities that someone needs to do the job, e.g., computer hardware and software, telecommunication networks configuration, length of an automobile, engine horsepower.

Not all requirements are needed to achieve a particular goal. We can become proficient in determining which requirements we need to look into in more detail.

Resource requirements help us determine how much time, staff, and other types of resources such as money and computers that we need to get the job done. It is critical to know how many resources are going to be needed to do a job. Often, it is possible to trade-off between time and resources. As an example, if it takes 6 months to design a bridge over the local river with 3 engineers, perhaps, if there were 5 engineers working on the project, it could be done in 3 months at a lower cost.

Project Management

When one attempts to manage schedules and resources to complete a project, this is called Project Management. There are methods and tools available to help us make these decisions. Two of the most useful are schedule charts that we call Gantt Charts, and activity diagrams (sometimes called PERT or CPM diagrams). Here are some examples on how to use these tools. We will do them by hand. However, there exists Project Management software to help us generate these diagrams. If we are working in a corporate environment, we probably need these tools. If we are doing this for ourselves, we can often get by without formal software programs.

Gantt Chart - A Gantt chart is nothing more than a schedule that shows when the individual tasks start and stop. We can add more details that identify the resources needed in each task or parts of tasks, and also to show how the tasks are dependent on one another. As an example, suppose that we want to build a large shed in our back yard. The Gantt chart might look like the chart shown in Figure 12-3.

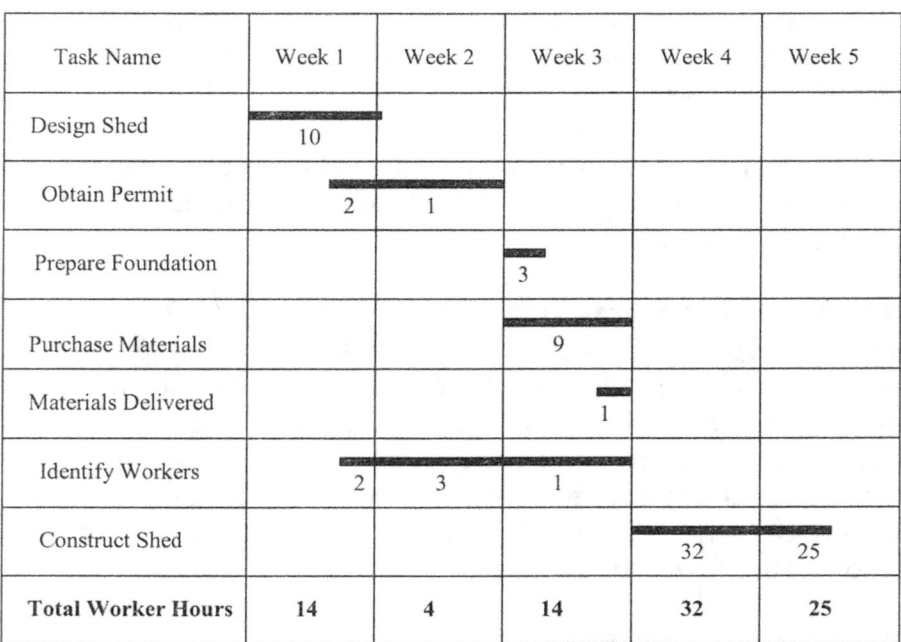

Task Name	Week 1	Week 2	Week 3	Week 4	Week 5
Design Shed	10				
Obtain Permit	2	1			
Prepare Foundation			3		
Purchase Materials			9		
Materials Delivered			1		
Identify Workers	2	3	1		
Construct Shed				32	25
Total Worker Hours	14	4	14	32	25

Figure 12-3 – Gantt Chart for Building a Shed

The tasks that need to be done are on the left side of the chart. The number under each time line (the dark line) indicates the number of hours needed for that task for the week. Hence, we see that it took about five calendar weeks with a total of 89 hours to complete the full shed project.

Activity Diagram - We can generate an activity diagram for our shed project by noting the interdependencies among tasks. For example, we should not begin our construction until we have a permit, hence Prepare Foundation is dependent on Obtain Permit being completed. Our project management activity diagram is shown in Figure 12-4.

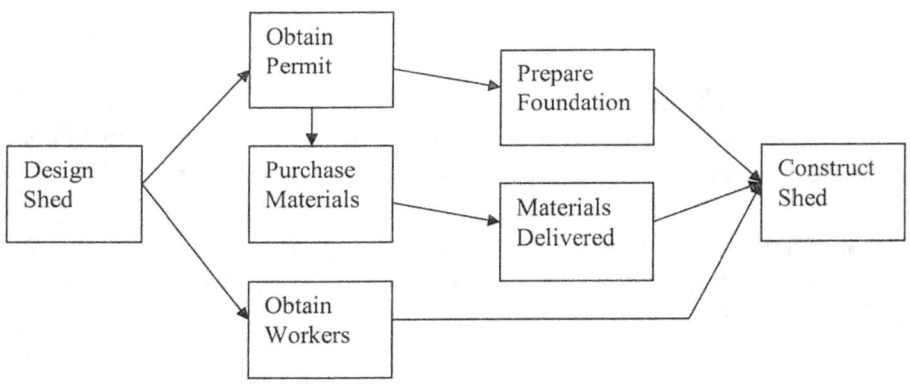

Figure 12-4 – Activity Diagram for Building a Shed

If we wanted, we could include the start and stop dates for each activity at the edges of the appropriate box. We could also include the number of hours needed for each activity inside the box.

There is one additional important point to be made regarding these schedules. There is one path through the boxes that controls the earliest date that the project can be finished. This path is called the "critical path" and should be monitored carefully if a specific completion date is needed. The critical path can change if we change something else in the schedule. In our example, the critical path is Design Shed – Obtain Permit – Purchase Materials – Materials Delivered – Construct

Shed. Computer project management tools calculate the critical path automatically.

Step 3-2: Is This Possible? – Let's Do a Feasibility Analysis

If what we want to do is complex, we need to determine if it is feasible to do. This analysis is called a feasibility analysis. There are several things that we should investigate for feasibility:

- Economic feasibility
- Legal feasibility
- Technical feasibility
- Time feasibility
- Operational feasibility

Economic feasibility means do we have or can we get the money or other resources necessary to do what we need to do. We should also look to see if it makes financial sense to do what we want to do.

Legal feasibility means that we must determine whether there are any laws or regulations that would hinder or stop our attempt to achieve our goal.

Technical feasibility determines whether there are any technical reasons (e.g., computer hardware and software, telecommunications limits, physical size of a device, etc.) that would impact achieving our goal.

Time feasibility means do we have the time to do what we want to do.

Operational feasibility means can what we are trying to do actually work, for example, can appropriate people or physical devices do what we need to do.

Each of these five things must be possible to do under the conditions in our plan. If one or more are not feasible, perhaps we can change our goals and plans to still accomplish what we want. For example, suppose our original plan called for us getting a Master's Degree in

Finance in two years by going to college part-time in the evenings. We might still be able to get our Master's Degree in two years, but it would require also attending classes every Saturday and Sunday. Or we could get our degree in three years without weekend classes. We have to determine which is feasible in our case.

In our enterprise environment, we may need to determine what new products are needed to maintain a competitive advantage. We need to understand:

- our marketplace
- our competitors
- our customers
- our suppliers
- our staff
- ease of entry into our marketplace
- costs, time, and personnel needed to develop the new products

Answering each feasibility question usually requires additional analysis and additional data. The gathering of necessary data is a key ingredient in any analysis, and data gathering should be built into the tactical plans. A word of caution, however, be careful to define as accurately as possible what data is needed. DO NOT attempt to gather all data available in the area of interest. This will take an long time and may jeopardize the total analysis.

Step 3-3: I'm Concerned – Uncertainty and Risk Tolerance

As we analyze our project to determine what the best solution to our problem might be, we are seriously affected by the uncertainties that exist from the beginning to end of our project. Some problems have only a little uncertainty so we feel that the outcome of our actions is almost sure to be the best solution. Normally, however, Our Systems World is so complex and the uncertainties so many that we are concerned that something bad may happen. Most organizational decision making is done under uncertainty. Never-the-less, we have to make a decision on how to proceed. This may involve making a risky decision.

Risk can be a strong motivating factor in an individual's or an organization's decision making process. Some people and some organizations are risk-takers and some are risk-averse. Our feelings will affect our decision making when risk is present. In discussing risk, we usually approach it in one of two ways. We might categorize risk as High, Medium or Low and use this breakdown in applying our decision making tools which were given in Part II. Another way to categorize risk is to give it a probability estimate. If we use probabilities, then we can do quantitative analysis to come out with weighted solutions (alternatives) as we did with the weighted decision tree in Part II.

We get our weights from analyzing the data from Steps 3-1 and 3-2, from our past experiences, from analysis of data which we have gathered, from weighting the advice of other people, and from using our decision making tools and concepts.

Step 3-4: This, That and the Other – Identifying Alternatives

As we work through our problem, we may come up with several possible outcomes (alternatives). We then need to reduce the number of these alternatives or prioritize them to help us decide on how we are going to proceed.

Below I discuss two approaches that I normally use to identify the possible alternatives that I will use to make my final decision. Keep in mind that regardless of the approach used, there is a need to identify problems as they arise. In performing these activities, it is sometimes helpful to enlist help from other sources. We can get useful inputs from other people, from data bases (e.g., on-line sources or articles that we saved), and from other sources (e.g., a library or corporate archive).

The two main approaches that I use to identify my alternatives are as follows.

Approach one is to look at the strategic goal and plan for the problem (project) at hand to get the high level view of where I want to get to. I then apply scenario analysis to determine possible outcomes and the intermediate steps in the project. Then I ask the following questions.

- Is each outcome for the project possible (feasible)?

- Will this particular outcome provide me with acceptable results?

- Does the outcome fall within my risk tolerance?

- Does the outcome permit changes in the project execution as I move forward and learn more?

- Can the project be completed within my time and resources constraints?

- Can the project be done with my current knowledge, capabilities and personnel

- Is there more than one good outcome that can satisfy my project goals?

This list can be modified and expanded depending on the problem and the individual or organization doing the problem solving. Again, the problem can be associated with an individual and his/her goals or with a large corporate entity. I then proceed to Step 3-5 to determine the consequences of the chosen alternatives.

Approach two is to look at our Project Plan developed using the outline shown in Figure 11-2. This contains most of the important data that we need to determine possible project plan implementation approaches and the associated outcomes. Using techniques that we have introduces in Part II, I make appropriate decisions as to the outcomes (alternatives) that I will use for my next analysis as given in Step 3-5.

Step 3-5: If I Do This, Will Something Good or Something Bad Happen? – Evaluating Consequences

Once we have identified the alternative solutions to our project, we can make our final choice by evaluating the consequences of choosing each alternative. Again, this may not be an easy task because of all the linkages associated within Our Systems World. The first order of business is to be able to identify and describe the consequences of each alternative.

As an example of what we mean by consequences, let's look at an example. Suppose that our corporation wants to take action to accomplish the following activities.

- Improve the information systems capabilities in our organization to permit us to process our business functions more quickly by a factor of three, and

- Upgrade the connections to our overseas operation.

Let's consider three alternatives

Alternative one is to take the existing computer system and upgrade the components to get the increased speed. This might require some retraining of IT staff, but overall little would change.

Alternative two is to restructure the Information Technology Services Department from its classic mainframe system operation and provide them with a new distributed computer system and new telecommunications capabilities for connection to our overseas operation. This would require retraining many of the staff and would probably require the replacement of staff members not able to operate the new capabilities effectively.

Alternative three is to outsource all of our IT functions. This removes the internal IT function and associated capabilities from the organization. This can save significant amounts of money, but would require the dismissal of most of the existing staff.

The consequences that result from these three alternatives are applicable to several of the decision making tools in Part II (e.g., Pro/Con analysis). Note that there are several other consequences that can be easily identified for this project – try to find others. We make comparisons among the different alternatives to see which one meets our project goals.

Step 3-6 – This Is the One I Want – Selecting Our Alternative

As we perform our analysis, we will identify one or more alternatives or options to solve the problem. Now we have to make a decision of which alternative is the best one for achieving our goals. This is a good place to apply the decision making approaches detailed in Part II to choose the one to implement

Depending on whether the decision is an individual or a team decision in a corporate environment, this will lead to a specific course of action.

If our problem is straightforward and simple, then we can take the actions which are identified in our analysis. However, if the problem is complex with many different actions which we need to take, then we will need to do more work to get to the desired results. As an example, if we need to implement many new capabilities to meet our goals, then the actions we take may require developing a completely new system. For example, if we require significant modifications of our corporate way of doing business, then our actions will probably include designing, selecting and/or implementing new organizational structures as well as a new information technology configuration.

DATA, DATA EVERYWHERE

Data, Information and Knowledge – What's the Difference?

As mentioned earlier, in performing our analysis we usually need to collect data upon which we can perform our needed analysis and make decisions. In fact, we would like to collect only that data which is important for our analysis and ignore data that we do not need. We can help ourselves if we understand the difference between the three terms: data, information, and knowledge.

When we talk about *data*, we mean raw facts or numbers, e.g., the temperatures in the major cities in the world, or the output of a device that measures the water level of the Mississippi River at New Orleans every 15 minutes, or today's movement of the S&P 500.

If the data is organized in such a way as to have added value over the data itself, we call that *information*. As an example, the profit potential of a new product based on the analysis of other similar products introduced under varying economic conditions is considered information. I further distinguish between useful information and non-useful information. For example, if I am interested in the prices of new cars, and you provide me with a report on the effects of religion in developing countries, although this last report meets the criteria for information, to me it is useless, hence I do not consider it to be useful information.

As another example, I googled Mississippi River and had over 16 million hits. I am sure that almost all of these hits do not apply to my Mississippi River measurements mentioned above. In fact, when I searched for "Mississippi River water level at New Orleans", I had about 540,000 hits, a significant reduction. I could further refine my search and end up with less data with more focused information that I need. So filtering our available data before we start our data gathering is very important.

Finally, we look at the concept of knowledge and compare it to information; we find that the difference is often one of experience.

Let's look at an example of what I mean by *knowledge*.

If you are playing baseball as the second baseman, and if you have the situation described below, what would you do and why would you do it?

- The bases are loaded
- There is one out
- Batter hits ball to you, the second baseman

You would almost automatically throw to the shortstop that would be running to second base. He would catch the ball, tag the bag and throw to first base – double play, no run scored.

Your experience tells you that the shortstop will be going to second base, so it is the smart thing to do.

But suppose that the ball was hit further towards first base and the man on first had a good lead and is fast, where would you throw it? There are several choices, but your knowledge of the game would guide you in making your decision. And a different player might make a different decision.

The point here is that based on our experiences (what we know, hence our knowledge), we will use those experiences to help us make a decision. These decisions may be different than our neighbor who has different experiences to influence her decision.

Now suppose that we have more useful information than we had before, could we make a better decision. Often yes! So where and how do we get that useful information? What about data that we had from previous experiences or analyses? Where is it? How can we find it easily?

Where Do I Find This Data Stuff?

Data is everywhere and it may be overwhelming to even know where to begin. There are several key places where we can get data (see Figure A12-1):

- Our files (let's call this My Database)
- Other people (personal contacts, blogs, on-line chat rooms)
- A repository such as a library, on-line database, corporate archives or bookstore.

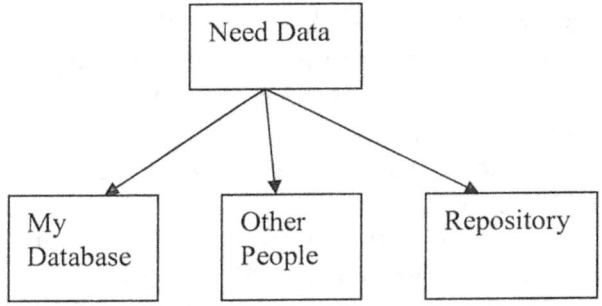

Figure A12-1 – Sources of Data

My Database

An important source of this data often relates to things that we have done or were concerned with in our past. We all have had experiences or learned something that can be important as we look at new challenges or new problems to solve. It is important to remember these experiences and to learn from them. They may not apply to all of our problems, but I'm sure that they can help us solve some of them.

Normally we just try to remember what happened or what we read. We have no structured approach to identify and use these old experiences.

In the corporate world, we often call remembering past activities and actions the *corporate memory*. Even in a company, this corporate memory can be volatile and lost, for example, when an employee leaves the company. Some organizations put in place procedures using what we call a *knowledge-based system* that is supposed to provide the corporate memory. We will discuss generating our own simple knowledge-based system below. If an organization already has its own system in place, and if that system is functioning effectively, the organization certainly should use that system.

We need to be able to identify the important things (let me call things *objects*) that we have encountered, and put them somewhere that we can find them, manipulate them, modify them, and reuse them. The reason I call them objects is to highlight the fact that I now include ideas and processes as well as physical things. The concept of modifying and/or reusing past objects is very valuable because this can significantly reduce the time needed to develop a solution to a problem. We can refine specific objects over time as we gain more experience. It is inefficient to reinvent the wheel over and over again.

As we look at our problem the first time, think about whether we did something like this before. Unless we have been organized and collected data in the past, we probably can't find the data we need. Then we have to determine where the best source might be – someone else or some repository. I'll get to those two scenarios shortly. But let's begin to generate our database now, not only for this problem area, but also for others in the future.

Building My Database – I have found that it is not difficult to make notes of important things that we learn. I write these in bulleted form.

I use bulleted lists rather than numbered lists because it is easier to cut and paste without having to renumber the list. I also like to group what I have written into categories. There are several ways to do this depending on how we like to think. Below is a short list of the categories that I use to keep my database up to date. We can divide this list any way we want to encompass all the aspects of Our Systems World.

- Personal
- Family
- Business
- House
- Financials
- Technology
- Miscellaneous

We can generate and maintain our database using folders in a file cabinet, on a database in a computer, in notebooks, or any way we want that can keep our data organized.

Once I select my categories, I further divide them into smaller categories (sound familiar? I am using my tree structure again). For example, the "Business" category can include the following as well as any other information from Our Business Systems World:

- Business
  - o Corporate Information
    - Mission, Goals and Plans
    - Organization and Internal Contacts
    - Other Management and Personnel
    - Corporate Products
    - Financials
    - Marketplace
    - Policies and Procedures
  - o My Projects
    - Project 1
      - Schedule
      - Reports

- • Personnel
- • Client information
  - ▪ Project 2
- o Reference Reports and Information
- o My External Contacts

If I am reading a report or article, and I find something of interest that I think I will use, I either summarize the key points or index the source and then put this data into the correct category in my database. If I summarize the report, I try to do it with bullets, covering only the key points.

It is time consuming to generate a database and should be done only if we intend to use it. Otherwise, just use the knowledge base in our head, other people, or an external repository.

Other People

Other people are a wealth of knowledge, but we need to identify the person that has the knowledge that we need. We can generate and maintain a list of people that we know or that we could contact if needed. This data goes into our database. An entry can look like this:

- • Jerry Smith; Phone: xxx-xxx-xxxx; Address: yyyyyyyyy St., yyyyyyy, yy
  - o Has done considerable work in maintaining aircraft engines
  - o BS in Aeronautics from Cal Tech
  - o Worked with him in June 2006 on Soar Project
  - o Good friend of Mary McDougal from work
  - o Has 3 kids and a wife named Jean

A Repository

My definition of a repository is very broad. It is something that maintains data. The data can be raw (nothing has been done to the data, for example the Mississippi River gauge readings that we discussed earlier) or processed (information on job growth in New York City). The data needs to be available to us. Note that some sources charge (sometimes considerably) for the data. The standard repositories that we use include sites on the Internet, libraries, corporate databases, and bookstores.

It may take some training to effectively use some of the available repositories. For example, if we do a general computer search on some subject we will probably get too many possible responses to be useful. Note: I did a search using one search engine on the words *new house designs* and received a response of over 85 million hits. By simply specifying that I wanted the three words "new house design" to appear in that order, the number of possible responses dropped to 560,000. There are also additional techniques in using search engines that could further reduce the number of possibilities.

For completeness, I will briefly discuss complex information system environments that exist in business.

Corporate Databases - There are many approaches and tools for gathering, maintaining, manipulating and outputting data and information. Database Management Systems (DBMSs) exist that will help to organize the data as it is entered into a database and increase the corporation's ability to access and manipulate data much easier than using the simple files that we discussed up to now. Corporate and government environments essentially demand that these systems be used.

Most business operations today are so complex that it would be nearly impossible to function without these tools. The use of a data warehouse to gather and hold information from many sources within the corporation and to provide the corporate decision makers with a multidimensional view of the corporation is often essential to the well being of that organization. Data warehouses can be used with other tools to help management make decisions. Some corporations use automated methods to capture the data that is needed.

What a World Wide Web We Weave

Although we do not need to have a computer or a connection to the Internet to use the concept of Our Systems World, having them can significantly increase our capability to gather more data faster. The key reports that I find on the Internet I generally put into my Computer Database. Those reports that I find in hard copy, I often put into my file cabinet or scan into My Computer Database. I work hard to keep my "hard copy" database limited to one file cabinet and a few bookcases. I also store my indexes and do most of my writing and analysis on the computer. Using computers on-line is a great way to find, select, store, manipulate, and keep important information. Access to search engines, fabulous data sources, and persons with interests in our areas are all available to us. Never the less, paper and file folders will work. The ideas in this book are centered on the steps that you need to take, not on the equipment used.

CHAPTER 13

STEP 4 – MAKING IT HAPPEN: *DETERMINING AND IMPLEMENTING THE SOLUTION*

Do What You Need, But Need What You Do

In Step 3 we identified the alternative that we are going to implement. If the chosen alternative does not contain any unusual or questionable properties, then all we need to do is to follow the action plan. There are a few activities that we should do as we take the actions identified in our plan. We should keep track of what we are doing by following our schedule and monitoring our resources using the charts that we generated in Step 3 (e.g., a Gantt chart).

However, if our problem is complex, we may need to perform additional analyses and activities to arrive at our desired outcome. For example, if our goal is to modify our corporation's way of doing business, then the actions that we need to take will probably include restructuring the operations (functions); identifying methods to acquire, sort and use information; designing and implementing a new IT configuration; and developing new policies and procedures.

If several people are involved, we will probably need to develop a team, ensure that each person knows what they need to do and by when, provide training, procure the necessary resources, and assure that the work being done is quality work.

Darn! More To Do

We now take our Action Plan as the basis for our doing what we need to do to get to the desired outcome. We are in fact going into a Systems Implementation effort in Our Systems World. There are a series of actions that we need to take to achieve our goals. And although these concepts apply equally well to managing a corporate project as to preparing for a dinner party, the difference is a matter of magnitude and complexity.

A list of steps that may be needed to bring this project to a successful conclusion are as follows.

- Step 4.1 – Procure Resources
- Step 4.2 – Select and Develop the Team
- Step 4.3 – Develop System and System Components
- Step 4.4 – Monitor Project Activities
- Step 4.5 – Control Scope, Schedules and Costs, and Project Quality
- Step 4.6 – Test Our Outcome
- Step 4.7 – Let Affected Elements In Our Systems World Know What We Did

Let's go over these areas in a more detail.

Step 4.1: Procure Resources

We can't do a job without resources. Resources needed can include personnel, financing, physical location, hardware, and computer software. The source of these resources can be vastly different depending on the problem and the organization. For example, in a corporate environment, the organization usually will supply these resources, although we may need to identify where in the organization the resources will be obtained. If the organization does not have the resources, then they must be obtained from external sources financial institutions, shareholders or venture capitalists, governments, family and friends, etc. We must keep in mind how obtaining these resources will affect Our Systems World, both in the short term and in the long-term.

Step 4.2: Select and Develop the Team

To get what we want done, do we need people to do specific tasks? If we do then it is important to identify what skills we need in each person, and then identify those persons available that best meet our needs. The skill matches often aren't perfect, but it is important that we provide the leadership necessary to get the job done. We need to make the best selections that we can under any constraints placed on us. External hiring may be necessary as well as possible outsourcing and acquiring consultants. Once we have selected a team, if any members of the team don't know how to do part (or all) of their task, then they need to be trained.

Step 4.3: Develop System and System Components

To achieve our stated goals, we need to develop our system and all the elements or components that go with the system. The system and these components can vary widely depending on the problem that we are solving. They can be physical systems, software systems, and even intellectual systems. We know the steps that we are going to take by looking at our plans.

If we are developing hardware and/or software systems and components, we can use standard design and development procedures, if necessary. We may need to purchase hardware and software elements and then properly integrate them to get a working system. As we do this, key questions regarding "Build or Buy" may arise, as well as "In-House or Outsourcing". Many studies have been done attempting to answer these concerns.

Step 4.4: Monitor Project Activities

Depending on the complexity of the project and the capabilities of the manager of the project (which may be you), observation of the project's progress and ongoing evaluation of the activities is necessary. I learned this on my first project management assignment. I trusted my senior technical researcher to do what we had agreed to, and let him progress as he saw fit. As we neared the project end date, I met with him to review the work and discovered that he had decided that a part of his work was more interesting from a science perspective and had ignored the rest of his project responsibilities. We two spent some very long days to get the project completed on time (and within budget).

Step 4.5: Control Scope, Schedule and Costs, and Project Quality

Controlling the Scope of the project is critical. By scope I mean just what needs to be done, nothing more. If the originally specified project scope turns out to be lacking, then a procedure to formally change the scope is required. For example, if the project is to change the way purchasing is performed in the organization, then you should not take on the task of changing the way that personnel are hired unless these two areas are interdependent. If they are linked very closely, then a formal modification of the project scope should be done.

In order to maintain control of the schedules and costs that we developed in earlier chapters, we should use the project management tools, e.g., the Gantt or Activity charts or other tools that we have at our disposal. We need to make sure that we have a handle on how much money and other resources are being spent and how the costs compare to our original cost estimate. We can do this by hand for small projects or on computer spreadsheets or financial software. The software can do many of our calculations for us.

As with any activity that we do, we need to maintain the quality of the results that we get. If we have designed some process or built a system, excellent quality is a must. In these cases, we can provide this quality assurance if we have the needed skill sets or we can get someone who has the necessary knowledge.

There are other areas not listed in the title of this Step 4.5 that are more or less important depending on the type of project that we are doing. Included in this group are controlling personnel and risks and developing quality reports or descriptions of what was done and how.

Step 4.6: Test Our Outcome

We need to look at the finished product to determine if it meets the goals that we set out to accomplish. Depending on the product, we can run various tests to see if it meets our goals. If it does, great, and we should move on to the next step.

If the outcome does not meet our goals, we need to take the action necessary to ensure our goals are met. We need to determine what is wrong and why. Then we need to determine how to correct the problem.

If we have a contingency plan already developed, this can guide us to the right approach. We may need to resurrect one of the other alternative outcomes. We may need to go back to Step 3 and redo those steps. Needless-to-say, this analysis is extremely important to do using the best people we have operating under the constraints of the project. It may be necessary to modify the project constraints if the correct outcome cannot be achieved under the existing constraints.

Step 4.7: Let Affected Elements In Our Systems World Know What We Did

In Step 3.1, we generated the user requirements that we try to satisfy during our planning and analysis phases. As we progressed through our project, we should be informing the users of the project's status and accomplishments.

Once we have everything completed, those users and other elements in Our Systems World that are affected by the outcome should be informed. As we pointed out throughout this book, every action we take affects someone or something in Our Systems World. If others are to interface with us and use what we have generated, then we need to let them know how to use this new capability and the benefits that they will receive. We may have to show them, train them, or send them information so that they can modify their Systems Worlds.

It is important to try to get these other elements to accept what we have accomplished. For example, doing business a different way can be a tough sell to many of the people involved. Even something such as moving to another city and another job needs to have buy-in by those who have been affected.

CHAPTER 14

STEP 5 – KEEPING IT GOING: *EVALUATING AND UPDATING MY SYSTEMS WORLD*

Is It Still Running? Evaluating the Outcomes of Our Actions

It is critical to keep up to speed in certain on-going activities to determine whether our actions are continuing to meet our goals. We need to update our plans and actions on a regular basis or unwanted changes may occur. We know that Our Systems World is constantly changing and with change comes new opportunities as well as new problems. So reviewing and updating our strategic thinking plan and certain task plans on a regular basis is almost a necessity to allow us to be where we want to be. Again this applies to individuals as well as to organizations.

One action that we might consider is maintaining our own database of critical information. Old plans, key information about Our Systems World, consequences of our actions, and contacts that we have are good candidates for our personal database. Some people today say that it is not necessary to maintain our own files and that we can get anything we want by searching the web. That is often not true, particularly when we are dealing with one of-a-kind or proprietary information.

We can maintain our own database on our computer, in corporate databases, or in paper files. Keeping our data up to date and purging out-of-date data or areas no longer of interest is a smart thing to do. Also we need to add to our database new ideas, websites, and reports that have a good chance of being important to us

If It Ain't Broke, Fix It! Updating Our Systems World

As time passes and our individual situation changes, the analyses that we originally did may be out of date and our plans may not be meeting our new needs and requirements. It is important to keep our goals and plans current so that we can adjust our actions to achieve our desired results. For example, we might have moved to a new city to take a new job some time ago, but the focus of the company has changed and we are not progressing as rapidly up the corporate ladder as we had hoped. We need to determine if we should quit our job and take another in the same (or different) field or just hang in there and readjust our plans to take advantage of new opportunities within the same company. Our needs and goals should help us make this choice if they are current.

In a organization environment, as the system that we implemented ages, do we need to upgrade our system to ensure that its life cycle is extended and that the system continues to be useful? Has the requirements in Our Systems World changed? We need to update our organizations goals and plans so that we know whether to continue to keep the system running by performing standard systems maintenance, enhance the systems capabilities, or replace the system. Sometimes major changes are needed – sometimes only minor changes are needed. These changes in our organization can occur because of many factors such as changes in:

- Business processes
- User requirements
- Organizations and personnel
- Funding

- Information technologies
- Product areas
- Regulations
- Ownership

If it is decided that the organization needs to change something in our plans or in our system, then we have to make sure that we understand the new directions that the organization wants to go or where in the system the needs are not being met. It may be necessary to just update some aspect of the plans and the system, go through a significant upgrade of the current system, or perform a new and complete project from planning through implementation.

The choice of what happens next depends on us, the project, the organization, and many other factors unique to Our Systems World.

INDEX